RESTLESS MEMORIES:

Recollections of the Holocaust Years

by

S. P. OLINER

To my family martyred on August 14, 1942, in Poland: may their untimely death, as well as the death of six million other Jews and five million gentiles, serve as a warning of what can happen again if we don't truly become our brothers' and sisters' keepers.

Cover designed by Jay A. Brown.

CONTENTS

ACKNOWLEDGMENTS

I am most grateful to a number of individuals who encouraged me to write this account and many of whom subsequently read it. Their sincere support helped dispel some initial reservations regarding its worthiness or interest for others.

I want to express particular appreciation to Ms. Lynn Crosbie who devoted considerable time to polishing, editing and re-editing my often disorganized, scribbled notes. She was able to make sense out of chaos. My special thanks, too, to James Hamby, Pearl Oliner, Carol Norris, Elaine Dallman, Jack Shaffer, James Johnson, Arthur Schwartz, William Helmreich, Rhoda Kachuck, June Elliot, Ken Hallum, James Carroll, Michelle McKeegan, Mona Skolnick, Sabra Chodor, Jean Bazmore, Shirley Ohrenstein, Carol Travis, and Paula Maslow who typed the manuscript and also did some additional editing; and others who gave considerable attention to the manuscript and made many valuable suggestions. Oskar and Hena Oliner, as survivors themselves who lived in the same region as I did in Poland, were most helpful in verifying the events described in the book. Jack Peller, also a survivor, helped me clarify some fuzziness of memory. Finally, I am most particularly grateful to Mr. Seymour Fromer, Director of the Judah L. Magnes Memorial Museum in Berkeley, who helped make this publication possible.

PREFACE

Restless Memories is the remarkable account of how a young Polish Jew — through courage, ingenuity, and luck — managed for six years, from the age of 9-15, to evade the German death machine that eventually ravaged his family, his country, and his people, the Jews of Europe. The author begins his story *in medias res,* at the point where he, a mere boy of 12, urged on by his stepmother and hoping to capitalize on his "gentile" looks, flees the Bobowa ghetto before its final destruction. From this point of high drama, Oliner — after but one chapter — turns back to tell of his life and that of his family in the pre-war years, so that we are half-way through the book before the chronological narrative catches up to the point at which it began. This structure serves not only as a dramatic device but as a means of impressing upon the reader that those who would fully understand the import of the collective Jewish death must know how the Jews lived as well as how they died. He who knows of Jewish history only the Holocaust does not know even the Holocaust.

The second half of the book describes how Shmulek, the hero of this non-fictional novel, lives by making himself, as far as possible, into a Polish boy named Jusek Polewski who works as a cowhand for a Polish family — a family unsympathetic to Jews, at that. Indeed, the early part of Oliner's book is a reminder that up to the very moment of the German invasion in 1939, some Poles did not have much love for the Jews, and could hardly spare a sideward glance towards the Nazi enemy at their gates. The book points out that some Poles were as brutal to Jews as were the Germans. Yet it was the sympathetic help of a Polish gentile peasant woman named Balwina that enabled Shmulek to save himself. Even in that darkness there shone a few, a very few, lights.

For Samuel Oliner, this story is a kind of memorial to his family, an act of filial piety as well as an expression of the nearly universal compulsion among survivors to bear witness to what had happened, to tell the truth about events that defied, and still defy, credibility. Anti-Semitism today takes two forms, both constructed on a massive distortion of the historical truth of the Holocaust. The first, or what might be called the right-wing form, consists of minimizing it or altogether denying that it ever took place. The second, or left-wing form, calling itself "anti-Zionism," seeks not to deny the Holocaust but to steal it by pretending that its original victims were not Jews but "humanity" and that it is today in prospect for just about everybody — except, of course, the Jews themselves. The German Nazis deprived Jews of their lives; the new anti-Semites seek to deprive them of their deaths as well. That is why every such testimony as *Restless Memories* is to be valued as a reminder of the terrible truth that the Jewish people, and they alone, had been sentenced to death for nothing but the "crime" of having been born.

Edward Alexander
University of Washington

INTRODUCTION

I was born in 1930 of Jewish parents in Zyndranowa, a village in southern Poland. Thus, I was nine years of age when the Nazis invaded Poland. My family was exterminated along with the other inmates of the Bobowa Ghetto in 1942, but I escaped. With the help of a Polish family I assumed a Polish identity and found a job as a cowhand on a farm not too distant from where I was born. Although I lived in constant dread of discovery and suffered many narrow escapes, I was neither beaten nor brutalized. Yet the memories of my boyhood haunt me and I have felt compelled to write them down and share them.

My memories encompass the complex family relationships which were the stuff of my boyhood, Nazi occupation and my life as an ersatz Pole during the war. While my story is an intensely personal one in that it is simply an account of what happened to one boy, I believe it also reveals something of Jewish and Polish life during this period. Unlike many other survivors, I lived the war years among ordinary Poles and thus had an intimate view of how some, at least, reacted.

Like many other survivors of the Holocaust, I feel an urgent need to bear witness to those years. I owe a debt to those who perished.

I also share a dim hope that knowledge of the past may somehow avert a similar future, despite considerable evidence to the contrary. Indeed, it has been suggested by some that given an already established historical precedent, it may be easier to try again in the future with any target designated for extermination by virtue of color, ethnic identification or whatever reason. I prefer to believe, because I have little choice, that those who remember the past will do all they can to prevent its recurrence; though I fear the future if we dare to leave it in the hands of those who ignore the past.

Finally, I want to honor those altruistic souls, gentiles and Jews alike, who risked much to help others. They were living testimonials to the human capacity to resist perversion even in an environment saturated with evil and madness. It is a strange irony of history that their deeds and names are more quickly obliterated than those of tyrants.

As this account goes to press, I must confess to some feelings of uneasiness. All of the people are real and some are still living. I have told the story through the subjective prism of a young boy's perceptions rather than the objective considerations of a social scientist. Any errors of fact or judgment need to be understood in that light.

RUN AND LIVE

Ester was my stepmother, my father's second wife. She was dressed in the rags she had sewn and patched and somehow managed to make presentable, and her face was grey and a little swollen. Her eyes frightened me. The dark rings under them made them look like holes in her head, and when I was in the house, they seemed to follow me, accusing me of something. I felt she hated me for some unknown reason.

Avoiding her, I crossed the room with the burlap sack on my shoulder. My father looked up from where he was sitting at the wooden table along the far wall. He looked right at me and his face was hard and expressionless. With him was my grandfather Herman Polster, my father's father. During those trying times, they spent their days going to *Shul* (temple), reading the scriptures and meditating. "God will save us," my father said, day in and day out; "God has always taken care of the Jews." My grandfather said very little. His farm had been taken away by the Germans. His shoulders were withered and bent over like a match that has been burned up, and he spent much of his time just staring at things, and coughing. He had asthma.

In the burlap sack was a rabbit I had stolen and subsequently killed, out in the Polish sector. Unlike the rest of the family, I had blonde hair; and once I got through the hole in the barbed wire fence surrounding the ghetto, I was quite free to walk about and steal things. This made me proud, and I couldn't see why the rest of the family didn't seem to appreciate my good luck. I dumped the rabbit in the center of the floor and threw the sack over by the door. Without a word, my stepmother picked up the rabbit by a hind leg and took it to a far corner. There she immediately started to dress it.

I waited for someone to say something to me.

My father said: "Ester, must you clean that animal here in the house where we live?"

Without looking up or stopping her work, my stepmother replied:

"And would you have me clean it on the doorstep for all the hungry neighbors to see? It would be a cruel trick to play on those starving with hunger." She was referring to the wandering, starving beggars, who looked into peoples' windows and when they saw food, they would knock on the door and beg for some of it.

He turned back to the table, where the scriptures lay open. My grandfather just sat and stared. I was never sure what he was looking at because he didn't seem to see anything. On the straw mattress along the wall, where we all slept together at night, Jaffa, my little stepsister, played with my stepbrother Shaia. Through the holes in the mattress, they pulled out bits of straw and let them fall from their little hands. Another family lived with us in this little room, and on a mattress along the wall opposite where ours was, a woman was asleep. She had two small sons.

"Where are the boys?" I said.

Without looking up from the rabbit, which was bleeding on the floor, my stepmother said:

"They are out with their father. He is a heartbroken man."

She covered the remains of the rabbit with a rag. In the morning she would scrub the floor with soap and water, if soap were to be found. Without soap, she would scrub the floor with water and sweep it clean with a homemade broom. On a tin can heated with coals, she began to cook our supper.

"This sort of thing I don't like," said my father, his head bent over the scriptures. "To see my family eat the food of the gentiles."

4

"Shmulek has brought us food for our bellies," said my stepmother, turning her dark, approving eyes on me.

"I don't like it."

My stepmother continued to cook the rabbit and my father said no more. My stepsister was named after my real mother, Jaffa, who was dead. What my father had to do with Ester, his second wife, was none of my business. She sometimes cried in the middle of the night, and in the darkness I heard her sobs. My father never cried. In many respects, he was like my grandfather.

Still standing in the middle of the floor, where I had dumped the rabbit, I felt hurt and angry. There was nothing for me in this overcrowded, crumbling, one room house, and I ran outside. Tears came into my eyes and I clenched my teeth. The alley outside the door was cobblestone, broken up in places and very uneven. It was late afternoon and cold for July. Moss grew on the dark wet stone. The sky between the rooftops overhead was grey. The buildings covered by tin, shingle or tar paper roofs looked as if they were about to fall in on me.

Along the sides of the alley were strewn bits of dirt and rubbish, wet leaves, black and soggy. During the early part of the day, children played games with the rocks. I wanted no part of such games. All of twelve, I was a man.

As I looked down the alley, the cold air crept up my belly and made me shiver. The smell of cooking rabbit came from inside the house. Such food or any other meat was rarely eaten in the ghetto and my mouth watered. More tears came to my eyes. I didn't want to go back into the house. This was a house of despair. Neither did I want to remain outside. I kept wondering why the Nazis made us leave our homes in the villages in which we had lived for decades and decades. The streets of the Bobowa ghetto were frightening. The men walked hunched in the shadow of the decrepit buildings and didn't speak much to each other. Mothers tried to find food for their babies, and the babies cried from hunger. Very few Jews would have delicious rabbit for supper. If a Jew was discovered in the Polish sector, he was immediately turned over to the Gestapo. If it was the Germans who found him, he was most likely shot on the spot.

Two months now, we had lived in the ghetto. Two months of hunger, sickness, and fear. The Germans said they were preparing a new life for us, and that the ghetto was only a temporary measure. Some people were even talking about resettlement in the East. This the rabbis and members of the *Judenrat* repeated and the Jewish people believed. The ghetto was surrounded with barbed wire and there was only one main gate. The Germans said they had our best interests at heart, and sometimes the heavy gate of wood and wire would swing open. Jeeps came through carrying young German men in uniform barely old enough to have hair on their lips. They had blue eyes and pink faces, and as they drove through the streets, they would take fun in shooting at people who happened to be along the way. When I saw these Germans, their pink faces reminded me of the flesh of swine.

A cold breeze kicked up and dust scuttled past me down the alley. The smell of rabbit made my mouth water. The sun had by now gone down, and in the strip of grey sky at the end of the alley I could see the moon. It was flat and cold-looking, like a round silver coin. There were no sounds that I could hear and the buildings were black. No one would bother to call me for supper. Yet I didn't have the courage to go back into the house. The cold air made me shiver.

Then there was the sound of a stone rattling along the cobblestones, and a man came around the corner of the alley. I didn't know his name. He carried his smallest son against his chest, and his steps were slow and weary. The slightly older son tagged along by his father's pant leg. We had lived with them for two months and even the names of the boys I didn't know. The man shuffled along in the deepening gloom, coming at last to the doorstep. Shoulders hunched under the ragged cloth jacket, he cast a brief glance at me. One of the reasons I avoided the streets of the ghetto was that the people you met spoke with their eyes. It made me upset and angry and I looked off in the other direction. The man climbed the doorstep and went into the house. His young son climbed after him and followed.

The rabbit was on the makeshift table. A candle lit what was to be our dinner. (Candles were hard to come by. I don't know how Ester got them.) The family, including the woman who had been asleep on the mattress, was gathered around the table and my father's head was bowed over his clasped hands. No one moved or said anything as we joined the table. I sat on a wooden crate I had found in another alley. My stomach was so empty my body felt weak. The candle was burning down. My father prayed a long time without moving, and the rest of us awaited his signal.

He said: "Forgive us, oh Lord, for eating this unkosher food, but we have to to keep our bodies from falling apart."

He raised his head and stared at the rabbit. No one made a move toward it. My belly was quivering and I had to swallow the water in my mouth. Then father gave the signal and the supper began. No words were spoken and the bones were chewed clean. One rabbit does not go far among nine people, and when we were finished my belly still ached from hunger. In a small sack in the corner, my stepmother had some flour for bread. We had to save it for another day. The *Judenrat* kitchen (a common kitchen for the poor) gave us some food, but hardly enough.

"I went to see the rabbi this afternoon," said the father of the two boys. His eyes were on the table. "The rabbi says the persecution will not last forever. God is just testing Jewish peoples' faithfulness to Him. He says the Messiah will come and that God will protect us." The man's wife got up from the table. She went over to her mattress and took the two boys with her. "He says we should pray and have faith that the Lord knows what He is doing."

"God will help us. He will protect us," said my father. Ester, my stepmother, let out a low sigh. "Our lack of faith He will forgive," said my father.

Ester got up from the table. She cleared away the bones and but the tin plates by the door to be washed in the morning. The candle was sputtering. During those times when I sneaked out of the ghetto in order to steal things for the family, I often took the opportunity to walk about the Polish countryside. This was done illegally, of course, but I looked Aryan enough not to arouse suspicion. And I often wondered why the Germans had stuffed us all into small places. Back in the ghetto, I asked this question of the elders and their reply was: "Only God knows why the Germans have taken us from our homes." But some did say that the Germans are a very civilized people who would not hurt the innocent. After all, we Jews have not done anything harmful to the Germans. We are guilty of nothing. That felt reassuring.

The candle sputtered one last time and went out. Chairs and wooden crates scraped against the floor and everyone prepared for bed. Tomorrow would be Friday, and *Shabbat* would begin. Before the war *Shabbat* was a joyous occasion. Shops, trades, and factories would close down early on Friday afternoon and people would start to cook special meals. Special breads and cakes would be baked. Pleasant aromas would come from Jewish homes and the time would be one of peace and happiness.

6

No longer was *Shabbat* a joyous event, but strictly observed nonetheless.

I lay on the edge of the mattress with my coat over my pajamas to keep warm. Ester was beside me. My father was already snoring and I listened to the soundlessness of the deathly quiet night. Even the babies, who could often be heard at this time of night crying in other houses, were quiet. The Polish peasants told stories of men covered with hair, who prowled on nights like this. With coldness and discomfort, I shivered. I felt as if I were being watched, as if someone were making special plans for me. And I prayed to God that it was Him.

Dreams were spinning wildly in my head. There was a gaping hole in the ground that seemed to draw me into its murky darkness. Somehow, I knew the hole was my mother's grave and it was waiting for me. The grave was empty and I was soaked with perspiration. Then there were loud noises and terrible confusion. There was an explosion and I awakened so suddenly I fell off the edge of the mattress. Outside the house it was still dark, and there were gunshots and people screaming. My father and the other man we lived with were at the window, staring out into the darkness. "The Germans are here!" said my father. Ester gasped and one of the children started to cry. From outside came the sound of deep, snarling voices: "*Alle Juden raus . . .raus*!" People were screaming right outside our door. Kids were crying.

Ester cried, "My God, my God, what are they going to do to us now? What are those Germans going to do to us?" There was a noise right outside the door and Ester started sobbing, gathering the children fearfully into her arms. My father ran outside to see what was going on. Immediately, my grandfather started praying: "God help us. God, what's happening? God protect us."

I jumped up from the mattress. Someone ran into me and I tripped on some twisted blankets and fell. Everyone was running around in the dark and before I could get up someone stepped on me. I got up and pushed my way to the door. Outside, people were milling everywhere, yelling and crying. Men in military uniforms were herding them with clubs and rifle butts to the marketplace called Rynek (city square). My father ran back into the house.

"The trucks are coming to get us. At the marketplace they're beating us and loading us onto huge army trucks. I guess we are just leaving, to where I don't exactly know."

"What are they going to do to us? What are they going to do to us?" cried Ester. I went over to her and said: "Mother, don't be afraid. God will save us."

"Oh, God! Help us, save us. What are they going to do to us?"

Still wearing my pajamas, I ran out of the house. The houses were one-story types, with sloping roofs, and I climbed up onto the roof and stayed there awhile, hugging close to the tar paper and listening to the sounds of cries and terror. The sky was becoming pink, the color of baby's skin. The sky was pink, and everything else black. I crawled to the edge of the roof and looked down. A woman was trying to hide her small child in a garden overgrown with weeds. The weeds were very tall and she crouched down, protecting the small body with her own. Then the child started crying. She shushed and fumbled to keep it quiet, but it was too late. The German hit her with his rifle butt, and stabbed the child with his bayonet.

The soldiers were going from door to door, shouting, "*Alle Juden raus!*" and pushing the people toward the marketplace, a square in the middle of the Bobowa ghetto. I was still in my pajamas. I saw a soldier throw a small child through a window of a particularly high house. Another soldier was dragging a woman by the arm. She was holding back and fighting him, begging him to leave her alone. She was

7

wearing only a nightgown, and her legs and feet were bare. The soldier yanked her ahead of him and hit her in the face with his rifle butt. I was crying quiet, hot, stinging tears and couldn't seem to catch my breath.

After a while, I got down off the roof and sneaked back into the house. My father was gone. Ester was holding the small children to her breast and rocking back and forth. She stared at me wildly for a moment, as if I were some sort of alien. Then she leaned forward and savagely whispered:

"Antloif mein kind und du vest bleiben beim laben." (Run, run away so that you will save yourself.)

"But Mother, where shall I go?"

"Go. Go anywhere. Hide. Hide. Hide. They're killing us all. I am sure of it now. The trucks are taking people from the parketplace to unknown places of slaughter," she added.

I backed away from her and turned toward the door.

"Shmulek . . . ."

Stopping, I turned back around.

For a long time she stared at me, her dark accusing eyes sending shivers up my spine. I wanted to run, I wanted to stay. I didn't know what I wanted to do.

"Shmulek . . . . I love you."

Bursting into tears, I ran toward her. But she pushed me away. "Go. There is no time. Go quickly and hide. Run away into the countryside. Save yourself." She had a premonition that this was the end.

Still in my pajamas I ran outside. People hurried past the end of the alley clutching their few belongings. In groups and in pairs, they hurried past, pushed from behind by the uniformed Germans. A young girl broke away from the rest. She threw down the bundle she was carrying and ran down the alley. The German guard saw her and aimed the rifle. Then, seeing me, he swung the rifle in my direction. I ducked quickly around a corner and just above my head a board exploded into splinters as a shot went off. Breathing hard, I climbed up onto the roof where I had hidden before. The flat sloping roof had been used as a storage place and I covered myself with old boards and pieces of rubbish.

The sun climbed slowly, so slowly, and the tar paper began to warm up and get soft. Gradually, the shouting, screaming and occasional gunshots subsided. All day long, there was the sound of heavy trucks. Hiding where I was, under the planks and rubbish, I felt sick. The dust made my throat and chest hurt, and the smell of tar paper hot with the sun made me feel sick. I drifted in and out of dazes, a sort of dreaming wakefulness, and flies crawled on my ear. Whenever there was a noise close by, my heart beat so hard I thought it would burst.

By late afternoon the ghetto was quiet. The people had stopped crying, the Germans had stopped shouting, the trucks had stopped roaring in the streets. The ghetto was almost a ghost town. A small, quiet breeze drifted dust on my neck from the boards that covered me. At one time, long, long ago, these breezes had been redolent with animal smells and alive with the sound of human voices; now, I felt there was no one left for the breezes to touch. Like blood going through my veins, a feeling of great loneliness filled my body, and I wondered if I were actually dead. Maybe I was actually dead, and my lot through eternity was to lie under these boards and listen to the breeze in absolute stillness.

Then I began to hear quiet sounds. There were Polish words and muffled laughter, shuffling and scurrying sounds. I slowly crawled out from under the boards, still and aching with an awful longing. At the edge of the roof, I looked down in time to see two Poles emerging from a house about half a block away. One man I recognized. Before the war my father had done business with him on market day. He was a Pole from a neighboring village, and emerged from the house with some little curtains in his hands. The other man I didn't know. He was dragging a ragged mattress behind him.

I waited until they had gone out of sight. Then, making sure no one else was on the street, I climbed down from the roof. My pajamas were a dead giveaway I was a Jew, and I searched through some houses until I found some clothing. A strange feeling crept over me as I drew on the pants with neat patches sewn on the knees. A breakfast of bread, baked under crude conditions and with black crust on the sides, was laid on the table. The floorboards were splintered but swept clean; and in the corner was a forgotten prayer book. My mouth was dry, my knees weak. I felt like a grave robber and prayed for forgiveness. The ghosts of the people who had lived there spoke to me with their unseen eyes. They seemed to say it was all right to take the clothes, that to keep a fellow Jew warm was better than clothing a rampaging Pole; hinting they themselves no longer had use of the material. A wooden shutter creaked outside the broken window and my body went creepy with fear. Hair rose on the back of my neck. I couldn't stand to remain in the house another moment.

Much as I wanted to run to my father's house, I was deathly afraid and took the other direction. The *shtetl* consisted of wood and brick buildings, with narrow, odorous alleys of cobblestone or just plain dirt. Some of the houses had tar paper roofs, some had tin. The roofs of tin glinted in the afternoon sunlight, and it was a cold sight, with no one, it seemed, to see it but me. Then I heard the sound of scuffing boot heels and peeked cautiously around the corner of a building. Six Germans, or Ukrainians in German uniform, were walking down the main street.

They split up and searched from house to house, cellar to cellar. Flattened against the wet, decayed wall of a building, I watched a soldier approach one particular house. Moss grew on the roof and moisture made dark streaks down the wood of the outer wall. As he pushed open the door, a young woman rushed out. She threw herself at him, insisting there was no one else in the house. He laughed and grabbed her waist, pulling her to his chest. Her body sagged and she didn't fight him, but I could see her eyes squeezed tightly shut. Then there was the cry of a baby. The soldier, who was a Ukrainian in the service of the German army, hit the woman and knocked her down, then turned and strode into the house. The woman jumped to her feet and rushed after him, but as she reached the doorway there was a pistol shot from inside, and she fainted right there on the doorstep.

I pushed away from the wall where I was hiding and ran. Bile was coming up in my throat. My head was in a daze and I ran and ran, stumbling on the broken and uneven road. Then I stopped and leaned against a wall to catch my breath. In front of me was an old shop, with boards nailed over the windows. My chest hurt, my knees were weak and I started to slide down the wall. Then I remembered the picture.

Of all my possessions, I valued most the picture of my mother. It was in my father's house. In the confusion of my mind, the picture stood out as very important and I was sure I couldn't take another step without it. The ghetto was a very dangerous place to be in and my stepmother had said, "Go!" but I simply had to retrace my steps. The market place was on a sort of plateau. It was eight to ten blocks of cobblestones and trees, shaped like a square. This area I avoided because it was where the Jews had been loaded onto German military trucks. Keeping an eye open for Germans and Polish looters as well, I arrived at last at my father's house. It was a sad looking structure, with low roof and rotting door posts. Saddest of all was the stillness of it. Swallowing my fear, I entered the door I had gone through so many times in the past two months. The room was empty. They were gone. Only twisted bedding and a wreckage of personal belongings were left. Some looters had been there already, it appeared. Something rended and tore loose within me and I sank to the floor. The small childish sobs wouldn't come. Instead, my chest felt crushed with the mature agony of an entire people. On my hands and knees, blinded by tears, I searched for the photograph. Nowhere was it to be found. I had lost my family. The picture of my mother I had also lost. She had died when I was seven.

As I wormed through hedges and crawled along the sides of buildings, one thought filled my mind: ESCAPE. As I neared the barbed wire fence that surrounded the ghetto, I saw a young Polish boy. He had a fat, white face and crooked teeth, and I'd had several fights with him in the past. Of course, he spotted me, and immediately sounded off: *"Jude! Jude* !" Frantically, I searched for a way of escape. But I was at the edge of the ghetto and there was no going back. There was no way out, either, for the gate didn't happen to be at this particular point in the barbed wire fence. Trapped, with no going back and no going forward, I rushed at the boy, desperately intent on choking the voice that was giving me away. The boy's eyes widened with fear. He dodged me and ran off yelling, *"Jude! Jude, Jude, Jude*!" looking for a guard and screaming a Jew was trying to kill him. Shaking like a leaf, I stumbled into one of those old broken down houses on the edge of the ghetto and hid in a small closet.

Very quickly it got dark outside and I spent the night in the house. There were dark and fearful sounds to keep me awake: the wind kicking garbage about, the sound of a board turned over, a door pushed open or closed. Once I heard a sob. Sometime later there was a small, thin laugh in the darkness. Loudest of all was the sound of my heart as I waited for some German, with his cold blue rifle barrel, to open the door of the closet. Only toward dawn did I manage to drift in and out of sleep.

Sleep was no more comforting than reality. It was filled with the faces of my family staring at me. And not just my father and my stepbrother and stepsister, but my real mother as well. Also Faye, my oldest sister, and Moishe, my oldest brother, whom I hadn't seen since I was put in the ghetto. All the while, the dark accusing eyes of Ester stared at me, as she clutched her children and said, "I love you."

In the morning — and how the rising sun made my chest ache! — I realized I should have escaped during the night. The golden opportunity had come and gone. Now the Germans were up and about once more mopping up the ghetto, and if I were killed, it would be my own fault. I was so scared I could barely open my mouth, and practiced calming down in case I had to speak to anyone.

Pushing open the closet door, I looked out into the room. Through the window the sun made yellow squares on the floor. The window glass was filmy and glared with sunlight. I sneaked to the door of the house. Pushing it open, I peeked outside. Mist was rising from the lane, which was dark and muddy. My clothing was caked with mud from the day before and the cool air made me shiver. The buildings along the lane were black and empty.

I left the house very cautiously. I breathed the air deeply and my belly growled. The ache of hunger was intense, making my feet numb and filling even my head with emptiness. As I stood there, wondering which way to go, a German suddenly came around the corner of a building.

"Halt!" he said, yanking the rifle off his shoulder and pointing it at me. "Who are you?"

"Oh, I'm not Jewish."

Astonished at my own voice, I waited, holding my breath and expecting the German to pull the trigger at any moment. He was a big man, with short blonde hair and teeth slightly brown. Looking me over from head to foot, he tried to make up his mind. Just then, another kid ran from the tangled hedge next to the house, crying in Yiddish, "Mamma, Mamma, Mamma."

The guard took off after him and I ran in the opposite direction. Very clearly the shots rang out. I ran along the barbed wire fence, then ducked down a narrow lane. The somber windows of empty houses stared at me as I slipped and skidded in the mud of the lane. Past a rickety wooden fence covered with vines and across a narrow foot bridge was the main road. Throwing caution to the wind, I raced across the bridge. Not far from the main gate someone had cut a hole in the fence. It was my luck to notice it and I ran through it and into the Polish sector of Bobowa.

The Poles were conducting their business as if everything was O.K. Dogs barked and wooden carts creaked along the road. A man in a homespun shirt was harnessing his horse. Noticing my hurry, he stopped and looked at me. "Hey, are you a Jew?" he said, making a step toward me. I dodged down an alley. Some dogs chased me barking at my heels and I stopped long enough to throw rocks at them. Then I continued through the town as quickly as possible without arousing further suspicion.

The country surrounding Bobowa was mildly hilly with villages isolated in the valleys. The Carpathian winters were extreme. Roads were poor the year around, deeply rutted and sliding off at places into ravines. It was now summertime and the roads were very muddy. The mud was cold and my feet were bare, brittle as ice and sticking with every step. I climbed the road away from Bobowa. I didn't look back. I wondered what had happened to my parents, and to the Jews of Bobowa. Where could they have taken them? Then I remembered the rumors in the ghetto about resettlement somewhere in the East. But where in the East? I kept thinking. Will I ever see my family again? I kept hoping. My mind felt empty and dead. Wild grasses grew green and spiky along the hillsides. Cattle were in the high pastures, and, as I trudged along, I wished I were a cow, with food and shelter and nothing in the world to worry about.

Toward noon I came upon a farmer digging a ditch along the road. He wore a coarse homespun jacket and wooden shoes. His face was brown with the weather; a rough, grey stubble was on his chin. Taking courage, I approached him.

"Please, sir, could you give me some bread. I haven't eaten in two days."

He leaned on the wooden shovel he had been working with and sized me up. I was certain he could tell I was a Jew. But I was too tired and hungry to run. Besides, where was I to go? The world seemed nothing but a cold and muddy road cut through hillsides of green and brown grass. The sun barely made a dent in the broad expanse of sky. When the farmer smiled, I saw many of his teeth were missing.

"Come to my house and I'll give you some bread."

We walked toward a farmhouse off on the side of a hill. A little trail of smoke came from the chimney and behind the house was a shed, called *stodola*, for the animals.

"It looks like the Germans have really cleaned out those wretched Jews from Bobowa," said the farmer. His footsteps were slow but methodical and I had to hurry a little to keep up.

"What did they do with them?" I said. "Where did the Germans take those Jews?"

"Oh, Jacek, my neighbor, told me they took them all to Garbotz."

"Where's that?" I said, trying not to sound too interested. The farmer squinted a little as he strode along.

"About fifteen kilometers up in the woods, not far from the village of Meszanka."

"And there, what are they going to do with them?"

The farmer laughed as if I had told a funny joke. "The Germans took care of everything," he said. "They shot every last one in a huge mass grave."

I stumbled and nearly fell and heard my voice burst out: "They shot them ALL?"

"Yes. Every one."

"But how can they shoot so many people?"

"They kept shooting them with machine guns all day long and some of them just fell into the graves from the planks that were put across the mass grave."

"Did you say some people were alive when they fell into the grave?"

"These poor naked bodies piled up on each other, both dead and alive were covered up with chemicals and earth. Some, who were still alive and were on top of the pile of bodies crawled out and ran away. Some peasant saw one of those people and he looked totally insane — as if his brain had snapped."

ONLY FOR A LITTLE WHILE

I was born in 1930 in the village of Zyndranowa which had no electricity or plumbing in the house. Before the war, my mother's father, Isak Polster, who was Herman Polster's brother, owned a small farm in this village. He was a tall man, slim and bearded. A sensitive person, learned in the tradition of Judaica, he looked stately even when wearing crude working clothes. Although the village was located high in the Carpathian mountains, near the Czechoslovakian border, the country around Zyndranowa was relatively flat. Small patches of woods provided lumber for firewood (main source of heat), buildings and fencing, and there was ample land for crops and pasture.

With the crudest of instruments Isak tilled the soil with his one-eyed horse. He treated his horse with respect and he sweated behind the wooden plow. At the crack of dawn he took the sacks of seed out to the field and at the day's end he was sunburned and tired along with his younger son, Mendel.

In a gray, large log house set among some trees he lived with my grandmother, Reisel. A wooden fence surrounded their yard. On this fence grew honeysuckle and sparrows hopped among the vines looking for insects and other food. A little way past this fence was a cabin built of logs. This was where my parents lived and it was here that I was born. My father owned a little land in the area and also had a general store in the village. He always had something to do and rarely did I see him at that early age.

My mother was a quiet, soft woman. She had a pleasing smell and a gentle voice. Every Friday, she would bake special things for *Shabbat*, and I took great pleasure eating her cookies, *rogelech* and *kichelech*. *Shabbat* was a day we all looked forward to. The very best of meals were prepared for this occasion and the whole family would sit down together. We ate and said prayers. Together we sang songs. As kind and thoughtful as my grandfather was, he couldn't seem to get along with his wife. They slept in the same room, raised a family, and lived their daily lives without talking to each other. If communication were absolutely necessary, they did it indirectly, speaking in the third person. Yet even they seemed amicable during *Shabbat*. No matter how unhappy or poor a man was, he always tried to get into the spirit of festivity at this time.

Exactly when my grandparents stopped talking to each other, I don't know. Nor do I know the cause. This was a topic my family didn't discuss. Most important to me at this time was that both grandparents loved me very much.

Living with my grandparents were their two sons, Mendel and Mordecai. With my parents and me, in the log cabin, were my older sister, Faye, and my older brother, Moishe. There was always the good feeling of having one's family close by.

Then one day my mother got sick. Mendel and Mordecai were both jovial and friendly, but I had the feeling something very serious was the matter. She coughed a lot and started to look very thin. At the time, I was about six. I ran to her beside and looked into her dark eyes.

"Mamma, what's wrong?"

She said nothing, but just looked at me. She was an angel to me — my mother — dark and beautiful. It was she who soothed my aches and I wanted desperately to make her well.

"It's nothing, my son," she said at last. "You go run outside and play."

"But Mamma . . . !"

13

She started coughing, and with tears in my eyes I ran outside. The sun was hot on the logs of the cabin. Strips of bark were curled out away from the wall. Dust was warm and deep between my bare toes and insects shone in the air. A breeze stirred the leaves of the trees alongside grandfather Isak's house and I couldn't believe there could be sickness on such a fine day. Mendel was harnessing the horse. My father came out of the barn with some straw which he put in the back of the wagon. Then he went into the cabin.

When he came back outside, Mother was in his arms. She looked light as a baby with her arms around his neck. He carried her to the wagon and made her comfortable in the straw. Then he and Mendel climbed onto the wagon seat. The horse quivered when the reins struck its back. Its brown hide twitched; then it broke into a slow walk, straining against the harness. Grandmother Reisel came from the big house wiping her hands on her apron. She had a rather square body with grey hair tied in back of her head and deep lines on her face. She stood next to me and watched the wagon going down the lane. Then she put her hand on my shoulder.

"Where are they taking her?" I asked.

Without a word she pulled me toward her and I buried my head in her apron. Behind us I heard footsteps and then my grandfather's voice: "I see they've finally gone."

"If Isak's good-for-nothing son, Mordecai, were here," said my grandmother, "he could have gone with them."

"Reisel should know her son has a mind of his own."

The sun climbed in the sky. The day warmed up, briefly, then quickly cooled; and the passage of time was dreadfully slow. When the wagon returned, my mother was not on it. Darkness had fallen. I was in the kitchen of the big house and the lamp on the table made shadows on the walls. My father came into the house and stood next to my grandmother. She would not look at him. He said, "I did all I could." Viciously, she pounded the dough for bread, her mouth a straight line and very hard.

"Where's Mamma?" I cried, running to him.

"I'm going to the cabin," he said. "The boy can spend the night here."

"What about the other two?" said my grandmother, still pounding the dough.

"I will send them over."

He left the house stomping his boots loudly on the porch. When he stomped like that it usually meant he was angry and we were in for a rough night. But now my mother had gone away. My brother, my sister and I were staying over here at the big house and my father would be angry all alone. I was very scared. No one would tell me what was the matter with Mother. All I knew was that she had gone away from home and I began counting the days until she would return. With a rock I made marks on a board at the back of the barn and soon the board was covered with marks.

At first my father said, "She is in hospital." Then he said, "She is in a rooming house in Dukla."

One day I rounded the barn and came upon Mendel and my sister, Faye. She had long dark hair and a chest as big as Mother's. Her eyes were dark as night, her skin smooth as the cream of milk, and Mendel often seemed to have trouble breathing when she was near. She was standing next to the side of the barn holding chicken eggs in her apron, and Mendel was leaning against the wooden rail of the fence. Faye was crying. At first I thought Mendel had hurt her. But then I knew he would not do such a thing. Farming life was extremely hard and he worked all day with the hoe and pick-axe. Sixteen hours a day he worked, except for Friday, and Saturday the day of rest. Above all else he was a gentle, loyal person who was always kind to everyone.

Then I heard Faye say the word, "Mother." With one hand she held the apron full of eggs. With the other she covered her face. Upon seeing me she very quickly wiped her face, and taking the apron in both hands, walked past me to my grandparents' house. Mendel turned around slowly. In order to see me he had to turn past me a little because one of his eyes had been damaged in an accident.

"What's wrong with Faye? What happened to Mamma?"

The muscles of his jaw bulged out a little. I could see he was upset. And not just upset as he usually became when around Faye, but really disturbed as if he had had to tell some bad news. I watched his damaged eye which looked white and waited for him to say something. With a sad look he turned his shoulder and walked slowly away.

Since my mother had been gone, Faye, Moishe and I spent most of our time at the big house. My father was there occasionally, but grandfather Isak didn't have much to say to him. Reisel didn't speak to him at all if she could help it. Most of the time she wouldn't even look at him.

It was at the evening meal that my grandmother announced she would accompany my father to Dukla the following day. Isak sat at the head of the table. He didn't look at Reisel. Neither did he speak directly to her.

"And will Reisel go alone?" he said.

"I would like to go with her," said Mordecai. He had a dark shaggy head that usually found its way into dark places. Certainly, he didn't spend much time in the fields.

Isak said, "When there is work to be done you're nowhere to be found. But let there be business in Dukla and you want to be first in line."

"I would like the company of Mendel," said grandmother.

Mordecai hit the table with his fist.

"Mendel this, Mendel that. If he is so good in the fields let him spend his time there. Jaffa is my sister, too, and I have as much right as anyone to see her."

"The table is no place for a fist and a voice raised against one's brother," said Isak.

"I, also, would like to go," said Mendel. "But I will gladly stay home and work in the fields."

"You see?" said Mordecai. "Mendel is such a good son. He will tend the crops!"

"I would like Mendel to go with me to Dukla," said grandmother. "The crops can wait for one day."

Mordecai got up from the table and left the house. I could hear his boots on the porch. "Mordecai!" said grandfather Isak. But there was no response from outside. I ate quickly to avoid the tension as much as possible. Faye was evidently not hungry. Mendel went to look for Mordecai and Faye excused herself. Only Moishe and I remained at the table with my grandparents. My grandmother said, "Come, Moishe, eat your food. You need good food to grow up strong like your uncle Mendel. Come, eat while it's still hot."

"Where's Papa?" said Moishe.

"Don't worry about him. He can take care of himself."

Mendel came back into the house and sat down at the table. He worked very hard and had a large appetite. I was the first one finished, and after waiting a few minutes was excused from the table. Moishe was also excused, and we went into the other room which was the bedroom. Through the wall I could hear the voices:

"Where is that black sheep Mordecai?"

"I don't know. I searched outside and called his name but he was nowhere to be found. Possibly, he went off into the fields."

"In the dark?"

"I don't know. The shepherds say they've seen him from time to time up in the pastures with peasant women. He's been seen with gypsy women, too, and the shepherds tell stories of his doings."

"No peasant would be out tonight. The moon is full and the peasants are superstitious. They are afraid of the evil eye on a night like this."

The voice of grandmother Reisel said, "No good will come of Mordecai's foul doings."

"Maybe he did have the right, though, to go to Dukla," said Mendel. "Jaffa is his sister, too. And we may not see her again."

Grandmother said, "Let us not talk of such a thing."

"But you know the doctors said there is no cure."

Grandmother said, "It is the fault of that stingy husband of hers. A business he has and land as well. And he says he can't afford anything better than a room in Dukla. Imagine shutting Jaffa off in a smelly room, separated from her parents and her children. If anything happens to her it will be his fault and no other's. May the good Lord hang a weight of shame on him!"

"But, Mother, she has a sickness for which there is no cure. The doctors have tried everything and there is nothing they can do."

After a long silence came grandmother's voice: "Tomorrow we will do what we can."

After this there was silence. Soon, the door of the room I was in opened and my grandparents and Mendel prepared for bed. Moishe was sleeping. We slept all together in this one room and I hid my face in the pillow so no one would hear me crying. I didn't know why I cried. Certainly, I couldn't understand why my mother hadn't returned home yet. Peeping up from the pillow, I could see Faye along the far wall. When she was upset her appetite failed her and she took hold of sleep with open arms.

Early the next morning the horse and cart took off for Dukla. On the wagon seat were my father, my grandmother, and Mendel. Mordecai was off somewhere. Moishe and I cried a little.

"Don't worry," said grandfather. "Everything will be all right."

As the wagon bounced down the lane, he watched it steadily with sad blue eyes. Then he went out to the field.

All day I waited for the cart to return. My grandmother had made some sandwiches for lunch but they tasted dry and harsh. Grandfather spent most of the day in the field. When he came back to the house he spoke very little. The morning turned into afternoon. Then it began to get dark. Grandfather lighted the kerosene lamps in the house. I waited outside on the porch. Insects made their night sounds and a dog barked on a neighboring farm.

Then I saw the cart, a black object on the horizon. I waited as the wagon approached the farm. In the dusk I thought I could see my mother sitting on the wagon seat. Oh, the joy that surged through my body! As the cart got closer, though, I saw the figure was that of my grandmother. It was then I had the terrible feeling. I wanted to run to the cart but my feet stuck to the porch. The cart pulled up in front of the barn and my father climbed down. He walked straight to the little log cabin. Mendel got down from the wagon also and walked around to the other side to help grandmother. She remained seated and he had to take her arm and gently urge her down. My feet finally let go of the porch and with trembling knees I ran to the cart. My grandmother was on her feet smoothing her dress. Mendel was leading the horse towards the open barn door through which thick yellow lantern light spilled onto the ground.

"How is Mamma? Is she coming home?"

Grandmother started to cry. She turned to me and said: "Your mother is dead."

I simply couldn't believe such a thing. How could one's mother die? How could she bake special cookies and cakes (*kichelech* and *rogelech*) for *Shabbat* if she weren't coming home again? I started to cry and grandmother reached out for me.

"My mother is dead. But that is only for a short time, isn't it?"

She put her arms around me.

"Yes. For a very short time. Everything will be all right."

And I went to bed that night thinking: "How short a time will death be?" At the age of seven it didn't occur to me that death was permanent. The days dragged into weeks and the weeks into months; and I still kept believing my mother would return.

CHEDER AND MR. HERSHEL

After my mother's death in 1937, my father decided to leave the farm at Zyndranowa and go to live with his father who had a small farm in the village of Mszanka. This was perhaps a logical decision. When he wasn't attending to business in Zyndranowa he spent his time alone in the log cabin. Isak spoke to him very little and Reisel ignored him as completely as possible. Father was the son of Herman Polster. And now that my mother was dead he didn't have to take any abuse from her parents.

Faye, Moishe, and I were to stay with my grandparents in Zyndranowa; and before my father could leave, the very important matter of my education had to be decided. I was seven years old and had not yet attended *Cheder* (Hebrew school). Most children — at least the ones from towns — started *Cheder* at the age of three or so. A Jew had to know how to pray. And to do this he had to know how to read. Also, a Jewish man was judged not only by how good a provider and businessman he was but by how well versed he was in the *Torah* and Jewish tradition. Being illiterate at the age of seven, my education was not off to a very good start.

"Shmulek will grow up to be a stupid *goy*!" lamented my grandmother.

I was in the kitchen of the big house having a crust of bread and warm milk. It was one of those rare occasions when my father was also at my grandparents' table.

"Then it is decided. He will attend *Cheder*," said my father. He was a big man with muscles on his chest and arms. Sometimes he looked at Reisel as if he would like to crush her.

"And where will he do this thing? There is no *Cheder* in Zyndranowa, as you must know."

"Dukla has a *Cheder*. I will send him there."

At this, Reisel looked right at my father. Her eyes seemed to have sparks in them, and I grew very nervous. Actually, it was all right with me if I never went to *Cheder*. I got along very well without the Jewish words and rituals one learned there. I would much rather have helped Mendel in the fields. The sound and smell of animals were comforting and I had no desire to leave all this and go to the town where my mother had died.

"And how will Shmulek get back and forth to this town, with his mother dead and you far away in Mszanka? Will he hitchhike on the roads, child that he is? Or do you expect Jaffa's parents to neglect the farm work in order to see to this matter?"

My father's eyes were black as he stared at her. His beard bulged and moved as he tensed his jaw. Then, without a word, he pushed up from the table and strode out of the house. Grandmother brought me another piece of bread and smiled.

"Eat up, Shmulek. That's a good boy. You must grow up to be big and strong."

Turning away from me, she walked over to the cupboard and took down the sack of flour. I watched her mix some bread dough. The kitchen was quiet. A breeze came through the door my father had left open. Birds were singing in the trees outside.

Not until next day did I see my father again. He had evidently been on a journey of some sort and was very tired. But there was also a certain lightness to his step. Once more in the kitchen of the big house, the kerosene lamp making his face look broad and pale, he said:

"I've made all the arrangements." The whole family was at the table: Faye, Moishe, uncles, grandparents and myself. Isak looked at my father and waited for him to continue.

"Shmulek will live in Dukla with a man named Mr. Hershel. This man is partially blind. He has two sons who look after him, so the burden of his care will not be on the shoulders of Shmulek. I have paid Mr. Hershel for Shmulek's lodging. Each day he will board in a different house."

Grandmother stared at him with hatred.

"And did you pay for these meals as well?"

"He will follow the tradition of *Mitzvah*. Each day a family will board him at minimum cost."

"Minimum cost! Charity, that's what I would call it," said grandmother. "Such a tradition is for the needy, not for the miser who wishes to save a few pennies. Did Jaffa rely on charity, too?"

"It is a good deed for which God will reward them, and besides they are getting paid," said father. "I have done what I can. I am Shmulek's father, and this is the way it will be."

Grandmother said nothing. Moishe had been going to *Cheder* all along, hitchhiking on the road. Faye would be in Dukla as well, studying to be a nurse. And I thought, at least I would not be alone in the strange town.

The very next day my father hitched up the wagon and we were off. I sat huddled on the wagon seat. Watching the reins strike the horse's back, seeing the back quiver, I thought it would be a nice adventure to handle the horse. But this my father would not allow. My brother, Moishe, had driven the wagon when he was seven years old, but my father would not trust me with such a responsibility. The thought made me angry. Also, I felt sick at leaving the farm.

Dukla was about twenty kilometers from Zyndranowa. The road was bumpy and I bounced around on the wagon seat. It wasn't very often I got away from the farm, and traveling through the countryside was exciting. The relatively flat land of the valley was divided like a quilt into patches of woods and fields and acres of potatoes and grain. Set among clusters of trees were small farms. From the edge of the valley rose the foothills and high pastures. Up in these high pastures I could see cows and sheep. Sometimes there was the distant shape of a cowhand checking his herd. The farms in the foothills were usually located near the slope of the hill or some other form of shelter. The winters in this part of Poland were very cold — so cold, in fact, that birds sometimes died in flight. The wind was like the edge of a knife. The snows came whistling down from the mountains and farmers took from the land what protection they could. Didn't grandfather Isak take special care to make sure plenty of wood was cut for the winter? I was very observant and knew a lot about these matters. My father didn't let me drive the horse, and that made me hot under the collar. For I knew a lot more than he gave me credit for.

Near Dukla we started passing the homes of town peasants. Most of the houses had thatched roofs. The walls were of mud and logs, and attached to the houses were small, lean-to stables. Some of the peasants had wells, circled with stones and sometimes covered with thatching. Through the town of Dukla ran a river. The banks were muddy and water reflected the sunlight. In the distance I could see a boy leading a couple of horses to drink. Along the edge of town a little way upstream from this spot some other boys were swimming.

The road leading into town was of dirt. Once inside Dukla we turned down a cobblestone street. People were everywhere. Carts were parked along the road and dogs ran about, barking and fighting over scraps of garbage. Some of the houses had tin roofs. We passed one that must have belonged to a very wealthy person because the stable was a respectable distance away from the house. Some of the poorer peasants actually slept with their animals. It had a tin roof, just like the house, and was big enough for horses on one side and cows on the other. I wanted to ask my father if a house like that might have running water. But he looked very quiet and I thought I'd better not bother him. We came to a crossroads and Father held back the horse while a peasant got his cart out of the way. Then we turned down another street also of cobblestones.

Presently we came to an old-looking house with wooden shutters and a crooked doorstep. My father pulled up the horse and hooked the reins over the wooden brake handle. He knocked on the door. We waited awhile and he knocked again. Then a voice came from inside:

"Who's there?"

"Aron. Aron Oliner!"*

The door opened, and standing there was an old man with a grey beard. His shoulders were stooped. The cap on his head looked ragged and in his hand he held a cane.

"I've brought my son, Shmulek, to lodge with you."

I watched the eyes which were turned downward and to the side. Shivers ran up my spine

"Shmulek, this is Mr. Hershel. He will be your landlord. I'll come to Dukla every now and then to pay for your lodging and board, and also to see how you're doing in *Cheder*. Listen to everything Mr. Hershel says and do not disappoint your father."

Petrified, I stood watching the eyes that couldn't see much. My father went to the wagon and returned with my few belongings. Then he climbed up onto the wagon seat and with a wave of his hand drove off.

"Come. Come, follow me," said Mr. Hershel, shuffling away from the door. I stepped inside. Tears were burning behind my eyelids but I refused to cry. Mr. Hershel showed me where I was to sleep: a cot in the kitchen by the stove. The kitchen seemed empty and cold. The stove was made of iron and covered with soot. There was a table over by the wall with a stub of candle on it. Mr. Hershel shuffled off to his room.

I didn't know what to do next, so I just sat down on the cot. The place didn't seem very homey without my grandmother. Sometimes she was hard, but always she loved me. For years she had not spoken directly to my grandfather. But she was a good wife to him, and he, also, loved me very much. I missed the good Mendel and black sheep Mordecai; my brother and beautiful sister. Even my father I missed. How long I sat on the cot, I don't know. My state of trance was broken by Mr. Hershel's two sons who came home from their work. They were tired and didn't pay much attention to me. They made some dinner and I had to take Mr. Hershel's to his room. As I lay on the cot that night I thought of the horses, cows, and chickens back home. There wasn't any part of the farm I didn't miss.

Just as the next day was beginning to dawn, a man came from house to house, knocking on the doors and calling out: "It's time to rise. All Jews get up and say your prayers." Having lived on the farm, I was not used to this sort of thing. Mr. Hershel lived in a Jewish part of Dukla, and Jewish life was very different from that

*Readers may wonder why my father's surname was Oliner instead of Polster: my father's mother was an Oliner who married my father's father who was a Polster. The wedding was a religious one and since they did not bother to register with the civil authorities, their offspring were considered to be illegitimate. Hence, my father took his mother's name.

of the gentiles. Everyone seemed to know each other; everyone contributed to the welfare of the Jewish community. Mr. Hershel's sons were getting ready to go to work. We had a breakfast of bread and milk, and I put a piece of bread in my pocket for later. That evening I would start the system known as "taig" — the tradition of *Mitzvah*. While I thought about this, wondering what kind of people I would have dinner with, the door opened and a small man with a wispy grey beard came into the house. He looked straight at me and squinted.

"Come on," he said. "The *melamed* (teacher) is waiting. School is to begin for another day."

Mr. Hershel's sons walked past this man and out onto the street. Mr. Hershel was in his room, and I was left alone with this strange man. He came up to me and took my arm.

"Come on. Hurry! We'll be late!"

Feeling rather helpless, I followed him outside. Waiting on the street were other children, most of them much younger than I, and the sky was still a little pink from the sunrise. One of the little boys immediately took hold of the man's coat, crying, looking back over his shoulder and saying, "Mamma . . ." Some of the other children ran ahead and I followed behind this man. The Jews we passed on the street wore strange clothing: fur hats and long black *kapotas* (coats). Some wore white stockings; and all were in a hurry to get someplace. From a side street came a man with two water buckets suspended from a staff across his shoulders. One way to make a living for a poor man was to deliver water to homes in buckets. He shuffled to a stop and watched us pass.

The road twisted this way and that, along houses that seemed to squat next to each other, cold and damp, blue smoke rising from their chimneys. How dismal city life appeared. The smells were garbage and wood smoke and people crammed together. Two mongrel dogs fought snarling over something in an alley, and a chicken that looked as if it had lost most of its feathers scooted across the road.

Finally, we arrived at a particular house and went inside. The room we entered was partitioned with some kind of drab fabric. Chairs were set in rows. The doorway to the kitchen was open and a woman was bending over placing something in the oven. A man came from behind the partition. He had a stern look and carried a switch in his hand. This was to be *Cheder*, and in the next few hours I learned some of the basic symbols of the Hebrew alphabet. The *melamed* (teacher) made up riddles to help us learn the figures. One boy, about seven years of age, was slow at learning and was misbehaving. The *melamed* grew impatient. In front of the entire class the boy had to pull down his pants. Then the *melamed* hit him on the behind a couple of times with the switch he always carried in his hand. I was the oldest boy in class, and this alone was embarrassing. Most boys my age were learning to translate Hebrew into Yiddish. To receive punishment in front of the class would have been more than I could have borne. With this in mind I learned very quickly indeed.

After *Cheder*, the man who had picked me up in the morning took me back "home." The other kids surged around his feet like a flock of baby chickens. Some children at the *Cheder* lived too far to walk, and their parents had to come to pick them up. I remembered my mother, her sweet voice and pleasant smell, and tears came to my eyes. Thinking of my father, a lump came to my throat. Somewhere in Dukla, Moishe was leaving his school and starting to hitchhike back to Zyndranowa. Grandmother was preparing dinner and Moishe would be there to eat it with her. My heart feeling like a stone in my chest, I walked next to the man with the wispy beard. When we got to the house the man told me he would not be by to pick me up in the morning. Now that I knew the way, I was to take responsibility for *Cheder* upon myself. I watched him go off with the troupe of children all eager to go home. For their happiness I hated them. With a heart of cold loneliness I reached for the latch of Mr. Hershel's door.

Then I remembered I was to have dinner with a Jewish family who lived down the road.

* * * * *

About a month passed. Then one evening my uncle Mendel showed up with the horse and wagon. At the sight of him my heart beat so hard I thought it would burst. He explained to Mr. Hershel I would be staying for a while in Zyndranowa. I thought I was to have a vacation and it seemed like hours before we were finally on the road.

A thousand questions rolled from my tongue and Mendel answered every one. It was simply a miracle to see his kind, smiling face. Every day I had prayed to be able to return to the farm; and it was too good to be true.

As we neared Zyndranowa I became excited. There it was! Darkness had long since fallen and kerosene lamps lighted up the windows of the farmhouse. The windows of the log cabin were dark and I was chilled by the sight of it. But the joy of being back on the farm quickly lifted my spirits again.

As soon as the wagon stopped in front of the barn, I jumped off and ran toward the house. The door was open and my grandmother was out on the porch. Behind her the lighted kitchen was warm and yellow and I could see the tall shape of grandfather Isak. My feet seemed to fly, and:

"Grandmother! — Grandfather!"

I hugged each in turn. The whole family was gathered in the kitchen. Even Mordecai was there and he gave my head a rub. Faye gave me a kiss. Moishe shook my hand, trying to act like an adult. Mendel came in from the barn and we all sat down to a dinner of stew. I had to relate all my adventures in Dukla. Grandmother was pleased to hear I was doing well in *Cheder*. Even grandfather seemed proud. Underneath the joy of the occasion was a certain amount of tension and at first I thought my grandparents had heard some disturbing news about me. Recalling some of the games I had played with peasant girls, a little bit of panic flared through my brain. Was it possible they had brought me home to punish me? Everyone seemed genuinely happy to see me and no one mentioned any bad feelings. After dinner Faye cleared the dishes from the table, with Mendel watching her every move. Moishe and I were excused for bed.

Burying my head in my very own pillow, oh, the thrill that filled me! Moishe was already sleeping, his breathing a steady sound in the darkness. I couldn't even close my eyes, let alone sleep. I wanted to run outside and say hello and goodnight to each and every animal, to the barn, trees, and the good earth. My father was the only one absent. I knew he was in Mszanka with Herman Polster. Just to have him near would have made my happiness complete. It gave me a great deal of pain to think about my father. I tried to change my thoughts to something else, and it was then I paid attention to the voices coming through the wall.

"I should think Isak's daughter would have made a match for a better man."

"A man does as he sees fit. It is the Lord who takes away."

"And Aron has seen fit to invest in a new marriage. To a woman divorced."

"It is a matter out of my control."

"Mendel, my son, please tell your father I haven't liked this Aron Oliner from the very start. That he should go to the marriage broker is perhaps business of his own. That he should so soon leave the memory of the mother of his children is my concern and it grieves my heart. When she was alive, he paid her little enough thought. But I am grieved it has come to this."

"Hush, Mamma. The children will hear."

"The children have a father who runs after a woman with land and a *szenk* (bar). A pity it is they must learn the hard facts of life right in their own home.

I didn't hear what else was said. My mind was racing, thoughts piling up on each other. Father remarried! Such a possibility had never occurred to me. And what was I to call this other woman? How could I possibly call her Mamma? The Polish peasants often believed in ghosts. I wasn't sure I believed in them; but I wasn't sure I didn't, either. And what would the ghost of my mother think when she learned my father had remarried? I buried my face deep in the pillow. Not for several months had I thought about my mother. Now, I wondered what she would think about this marriage. I also wondered if she was in heaven.

After a while I felt better. From my sorrow rose a bubble of excitement and I began to look at the situation in a new light. Still troubled at the thought of having a new mother, I was at the same time a little excited at having a new member of the family. As I went to sleep, I was confused with despair and hope, and very strange dreams filled the night.

A few days later my father showed up at the farm in Zyndranowa. He had come for some things from the log cabin, and my grandparents greeted him cooly. I found out he lived in Bielanka, which was a few kilometers west of Mszanka, on some property his new wife happened to own. It was in Mszanka where Herman Polster lived and I remembered it as a warm, friendly place. Herman Polster was my grandfather on my father's side of the family and I had seen him only a couple of times. I began thinking that my mother and my father were first cousins. I was wondering how they met and if they were ever happy together.

Father asked if any of us children would like to see our stepmother. What a strange feeling the word "stepmother" gave me! Right away, I was sure I wouldn't like her. Father looked at Faye. She, in turn, glanced at grandmother Reisel, then said she couldn't because she was to begin nurses' training in Dukla. Then my father looked at Moishe. He hung his head and said he couldn't go either because the year was getting on toward fall and he had promised to help Mendel harvest the grain.

My father didn't say anything, but I could see a red coal of anger was deep down inside him. His beard seemed more bristly than usual. And it wasn't really Faye or Moishe at whom he was angry. He shot a glance at Reisel that gave me the shivers. Then at last he looked at me.

His expression was one of, "O.K., you, too, can say you don't want to go." But quite to the contrary, I was anxious to visit this place Bielanka. Perhaps I would get a chance to visit Herman Polster. Or maybe I would get to see Gorlice, a big town not too far away from grandfather Herman's farm.

So I said, "Sure, I'll go with you."

Both Faye and Moishe gave me startled glances. Even my father looked surprised. Grandmother said:

"What about *Cheder*: How will you continue his education in Bielanka, a village smaller than Zyndranowa?"

My father said, "That's no problem. There is a *Cheder* in Gorlice and I will make sure he goes every day."

"Perhaps you will put him in a rooming house?"

"I will do as I see fit."

I packed my changes of clothing and said goodbye to everyone. Faye seemed very tense. Moishe stood off a ways. Grandmother cried a little and Isak shook my hand as if I were a man. That made me feel very proud. I climbed up on the wagon seat and looked back one last time to wave. They all stood in a group, and I was very aware they were my family. The wind stirred the leaves of the trees along the house and I waved as the wagon started off. The warm bodies of my family waved back and I was torn with love for them all.

My father held the reins quietly as the wagon bumped along the road. He wore a black hat and a dark coat. His black beard and white cheeks made him look like an animal snug down in its fur. But a large animal – a bear, perhaps. I couldn't wait until my beard would grow. I couldn't wait until the time I could just hitch up the horse and drive somewhere –when I was a man. Then, I thought, my life would begin.

"How was *Cheder*?"

"Very good. I learned the Hebrew letters quickly. They look like animals, you know, and I memorized them in no time."

"Hmmm. And how is Mr. Hershel, your landlord?"

"He stays in his room all the time. In the morning I have to take him breakfast and clean the house. Mr. Hershel's sons leave early in the morning for work and don't return until evening. Each night I have dinner in the home of a Jewish family, a different family each night. When I am at the home of Mr. Hershel I have the house pretty much to myself."

What I didn't tell him was the loneliness – the awful loneliness – that caved in each night as I went to bed. In the mornings, I watched the Jewish mothers and fathers bring their children to *Cheder*. In the afternoon these parents returned to take their children back home At school I had a reputation for fighting and it was these children with whom I got into fights most often. I wanted to hurt them in some way because they were happy; because they had mothers and fathers who picked them up.

My father said, "Do you like living with grandfather Isak?"

"Yes I do. They are very kind."

"But they never speak to each other. Doesn't that bother you?"

"They are very good to Faye and Moishe and me."

"For twenty years they have not spoken to each other and not even I know the reason why But Reisel's a very strange woman. She has told you stories of me?"

"No. Why should she say anything about you?"

"What has she said that would make your sister and brother not want to visit their stepmother in Bielanka?"

"I don't know."

"Tell me. I am your father and should know these things!"

"I don't know what you're talking about. Grandmother and grandfather are always very friendly."

"But not where I am concerned. I can see that. I would only like to know what she says. I know she blames me for your mother's death, but that couldn't be helped: she blames me for not getting the best doctors to take care of her during her illness. She had tuberculosis. There was nothing the doctors could do. It was just a matter of time, and your grandmother doesn't seem to realize that. She isn't **always** so smart and I would just like to know what she has to say when my back is turned."

Shaking all over I huddled on the seat. My father got quiet again and gave the reins a flick. Gradually, I calmed down. From Zyndranowa to Bielanka was over forty kilometers and we arrived at my stepmother's farm late in the night.

There was a corral and a small shed for animals. Next to the house was the *szenk*, or bar, where peasants drank Jewish whiskey during the daytime. The windows of the house were flooded with light. When my father opened the kitchen door, the light fell on my face and I saw standing by the stove the woman who was my stepmother. She had dark hair and dark eyes, like my dead mother. But she was younger than my mother had been and her kitchen didn't smell nearly as good as had my mother's. She smiled and came over to me, stooping with arms outstretched. The greeting was very warm and I thought perhaps I would like this strange woman after all.

Then, from the adjoining room walked the most frightening man I had ever seen. His face shook from side to side and his eyes rotated around in circles. "Hello, how are you?" he said to me, extending his hand and rolling his eyes. I hid behind the skirts of my stepmother. The man walked around her, bending over and extending his hand. "Hello, how are you?" he said, shaking his head. I started to cry.

"This is my brother," said the woman behind whose skirts I hid. "He is married and lives in Gorlice. From time to time he visits me. There is no reason to be afraid."

And I noticed she gave me a strange look, as if she felt badly that I didn't like her brother. He tried to be friendly. I wanted to like him and please my stepmother, but it was no use: he was so frightening I couldn't bear to look at him, and the next day I asked my father to take me back to Zyndranowa. Of course, such a thing was positively out of the question. And I was stuck in Bielanka for several months.

Once again the problem of *Cheder* came up. I would have been perfectly happy not to attend at all. But social pressure was very strong and my father had an obligation to fulfill. Bielanka had no *Cheder*. Nor did Mszanka where grandfather Herman lived. The nearest large town was about ten kilometers away. The name of this town was Gorlice and it was there that I attended *Cheder*.

* * * * *

Happy was the day when I once more set eyes upon Zyndranowa. I was about eight years old and made the trip alone, hitchhiking on the road. I had quarreled with my father and was sort of running away from home. Actually, I was running from one home to another. One did not have to stay with one's father, and I left a barely legible note for him saying I would be at grandfather Isak's.

The problem with my father was that he was not very openminded. He was a good businessman and hard worker; he learned well what was offered in the *Cheder*, which teaches the *Torah* and Jewish tradition. But beyond that, he didn't know too much. All I did was ask him why the Polish gentiles didn't believe in the *Torah*.

"Why do you want to know?" he said, writing some notes with a pencil on a piece of paper. Rarely did he pay much attention to me. I sometimes had the feeling I could die noisily right in front of him and he wouldn't notice.

"I just was curious."

"Are you getting Christian notions in your head? Is it a *goy* (a dumb gentile) I'm raising you to be?"

"No. I was just curious. Honest. It just seems strange the Poles sometimes don't even know what the *Torah* is."

My father put down the pencil and glanced at me.

"Well, you just stick to your lessons. The Poles are not the chosen people of God. You leave them alone and maybe they'll leave you alone. And remember, it was curiosity that brought deceitfulness into the world."

After that I wouldn't speak to him. I didn't get along with my stepmother. She called me lazy when actually I did as much work as anyone; and you might say the argument with my father was the final straw that broke my willingness to stay at Bielanka.

When once more I saw the faces of Isak and Reisel, my heart bounced into flight. Faye was home from Dukla and Moishe asked me alot of questions about Bielanka. Then he decided he wanted to visit our stepmother. It seemed odd to see him go back to where I had just come from.

Grandfather Isak's farm was pretty much the same as ever. The harsh winter was past and the trees were putting forth their new buds. After a time of ice and snow the earth was beginning to warm to the sun; and grandfather and Mendel spent all day working in the fields, plowing the earth and planting grain. I helped a little, but for the most part my time was free and I spent many days just soaking up the warm spring sun. The earth was warming all around me; cows were calving and birds were nesting in the grasses. During this time of restfulness I began to pay more attention to uncle Mordecai.

For some reason this man intrigued me. He was the black sheep of the family. Even when he helped with the farmwork his efforts were't appreciated. My grandfather would say: "Look how hard Mendel works and how lazy you are." Grandfather Isak wasn't to be pleased by this wayward son. Consequently, Mordecai did only what he wanted to do. As he had no love for the soil, he generally ended up roaming the countryside. For hours, sometimes days, he would be gone away from the farm. When I asked him what he did during these periods of time, he just grinned. The shepherds from the high pastures said he made love to peasant women.

Of course, I understood if a peasant girl wanted to meet a man who wasn't in her family it was done in the woods or high pastures. Also, it was done during the daytime. The houses of most peasants consisted of two rooms. One of these was a bedroom where all the members of the family slept, either separately or together. The town gossips referred to such meetings as love-making. I was about eight years old at the time and didn't quite understand what was meant by love-making, but the idea of Mordecai meeting a peasant girl in the fields filled me with excitement. My grandparents did not approve of these meetings, which made them all the more exciting for me. Several times I had seen the naked chest of my sister Faye. I was sure "making love" had something to do with a woman's chest, and the thought of Mordecai doing this thing filled me with many emotions, none of which I was absolutely certain. And very quickly I came to adore Mordecai. Why my grandparents would disapprove of his activities was beyond my comprehension. Fascinating man that he was, he could do no wrong, and the good Mendel began to seem like a dull person indeed beside this black sheep.

As I followed him around the farm and watched him I noticed that, like Mendel, he seemed to like Faye very much. She was a nice girl — very kind to me — and I certainly could understand why someone would like her. Also, with black hair, dark eyes, and lips like a ripe fruit, she was pleasant to look at. But I couldn't understand why Mendel would blush and get tongue-tied in her presence. Mordecai didn't blush; but he would get quick eyes: they would glance at her, then dart off somewhere else, back and forth, from Faye to somewhere else they would go. The difference between Mordecai and Mendel was that Mordecai usually avoided Faye if he had any choice in the matter. If he saw her walking toward him, he might very well go off in another direction.

Apparently, he didn't avoid other women, and the shepherds said he met with gypsies as well as peasants. There was a gypsy encampment just outside of Dukla. In a hollow on the side of a hill, they built their shanty town. One day I rode with Mendel to get farm supplies in Dukla. On the way home he whipped up the horse as we passed the gypsy camp. The frown on his face showed exactly how he felt and I didn't ask any dumb questions. Gypsy music hung in the air and the smell of oil and cooking meat. I looked back over my shoulder and there were the huts made of wood, sod, and canvas. A woman with dark hair tied back was tending a fire. Large silver earrings hung down her neck. Her eyes were dark, her mouth broad with thick lips. As she bent over the fire her blouse fell forward. I could see the flesh of her breasts, and in my imagination Mordecai was touching them. Gypsy smoke hung like magic in the air.

It just so happened Mordecai was at the farm when we got there. He was sitting on the corral fence by the barn talking to Faye. Mendel had the same frown as when we passed the gypsy camp. I jumped off the wagon. Mendel got down also and led the horses into the barn. Faye walked to the house and I went over to the corral fence where Mordecai was sitting.

"Hi."

He looked at me, then grinned in a lopsided fashion.

"Hi."

From the ground I picked up a splinter and twisted it in half. Then I looked at him. When our eyes met he looked off toward the horizon.

"We passed the gypsy camp outside Dukla."

Mordecai seemed amused. Unlike Mendel, Mordecai shaved his beard, and I could see his smooth jaw working.

"Say, I was wondering . . ."

"What's that?"

"Why don't the Poles like gypsies?"

"Well, if the gypsies see a chicken or something they like, they simply take it and cook it for dinner without asking the owner's permission."

"But don't they sometimes work for the Poles?"

"Don't who work for the Poles?"

I said, "The gypsies!"

"Sure. They get odd jobs and such. But just the same, the Poles don't treat them very well."

"Because the gypsies steal?"

"Who knows? Maybe. On the other hand, maybe the gypsies steal from the Poles because the Poles don't treat them well. The rabbi seems to know everything, so maybe you should go ask him."

Mordecai wasn't very religious and his making fun didn't surprise me. But I was serious. There were many questions I had about the gypsies. Why did the gypsies cast such a spell over him, for it seemed such a strange life, living in wagons and shanty towns and simply packing up whenever you wanted to leave. Such a life I thought I'd like. No farm chores to do, no *Cheder* to attend — what a way to live! The shepherds said Mordecai played games and laughed with the gypsy women, and this was the sort of thing I thought I'd like to do.

"Are the gypsy women beautiful?"

Mordecai looked at me shrewdly. "What do you know about 'beautiful'? Doesn't your grandmother want you to grow up to be like your good uncle Mendel? Or has she stopped speaking to you also?"

"Of course grandmother talks to me."

Mordecai laughed, sliding off the rail fence. Still laughing, he walked around the barn. He seemed in a hurry to get somewhere and I had to run a little to catch up. He stopped and waited for me.

He said, "Hey, you know what? Your grandparents are in the kitchen 'discussing' some important matters. Why don't you go and hear what they have to say?"

"But no one ever talks serious matters when I'm around."

"Well, go and spy on them," said Mordecai, bending over and whispering in my ear: "Do it for me, O.K.? Go listen to what they have to say and then tell me about it."

His eyes were dark and dancing and he had the lopsided grin. I had no idea why he would want me to spy on my grandparents. But the idea of doing something for Mordecai thrilled me and I determined to do a good job. Like a flash I ran out of the barn. Circling around the house, I crawled through some bushes up to the kitchen window, which was slightly open.

There were my grandparents, all right. My grandmother sat at one end of the table, my grandfather at the other. He didn't look at her, she didn't look at him. They were alone. For about five minutes I waited and not a single word was spoken. Finally, my grandmother said:

"Isak should know I think it's about time for Shmulek to return to *Cheder*. He did very well while he was in Dukla last time. But his education is not yet complete."

Grandfather said nothing. On the table in front of him was a clay mug. His back was very straight in the chair. Flies were crawling on my leg and I held my breath for fear of giving myself away. For perhaps another five minutes I waited. Then Faye walked into the kitchen.

"Tell your grandmother arrangements will be made. Tell her I now have to go back to work."

While Faye relayed the message, I crawled out of the bushes along the house and ran to find Mordecai. Why the subject of my going to *Cheder* would interest him, I had no idea. But he had asked me to spy and I was anxious to please him.

First I checked the barn, the two horses were there in their stalls munching some oats and stirring the straw bedding with their feet. They looked at me with those big, brown eyes and wrinkled up their noses, and I couldn't resist rubbing their necks. In another stall was the cow, its wet nose shiny. I patted the cow, too, then ran to the back of the barn where the hay was piled. Mordecai was the kind of person who could be anywhere.

I ran back outside, coming into the bright springtime sunlight. A sparrow flew up from the ground with string in its beak to make a nest. The air was cool, fresh

28

and invigorating. I checked along the corral fence and out in back of the barn, scanning the fields and woods and the houses and barns of grandfather Isak's neighbors.

Dreadfully discouraged, feeling I had somehow been tricked by my uncle, I sat on the doorstep of the log cabin. Where he could possibly be was a complete mystery to me. Of course, he could be visiting a neighbor, he could have gone off on one of his hikes. But why then would he have asked me to spy on my grandparents? If his purpose had been to trick me, where could he have gone that he didn't want me to follow?

Then I thought of the cellar. Most Poles, and Jews as well, had cellars of brick or rock or dried mud. They might be under the house, or they might be dome-shaped structures dug into the ground somewhere away from the house with steps leading down. Certain things like butter and milk had to be kept cool during the summers. Potatoes and other supplies had to be kept warm during the winters. Cellars kept an ideal temperature for these items and were therefore rather a necessity.

My grandparents' cellar happened to be located under the house. I went around the honeysuckle-covered fence and approached the back of the house, where the cellar door opened out. The door was open a crack. In back of me was a large field and then woods. I could see the village of Zyndranova, and the farms and houses of neighbors were in plain sight. I stood among the trees next to the house. Next to the cellar door were some bushes. For a moment I stopped to look at the fresh new green of the tree leaves. A cool breeze moved through these leaves and I quietly pushed open the cellar door. Some instinct warned me to be cautious, and I waited silently as my eyes adjusted to the darkness. What I then saw made my heart skip a beat and seem to stop dead still.

There on the soft earth of the cellar floor was Natzcka, the most beautiful unmarried woman in all of Zyndranowa. Her skirt was up around her waist, making plainly visible the dark area between her legs. Her blouse was completely off, her chest exposed. All this I saw even before I realized Mordecai was on top of her. In the next few minutes I got a lesson I would never forget. It had never occurred to me men and women could possibly do such things. At first, I thought Mordecai and this woman were strange, that they were doing something unnatural. After a while they laughed together. They seemed happy and I was very troubled about it all.

Feeling it very important I not be discovered, I slipped out of the cellar and pulled the door shut. Troubled as I was, I had seen something which made some of the gossip around Zyndranowa make more sense than it ever had before. From thinking Mordecai and Natzcka were strange for doing to each other what they had, I came to the realization such practices were common. Mordecai wasn't the only one who made love in the woods! Furthermore, I had witnessed the love-making of animals and knew this was how the animals were bred and had their young. What Mordecai and Natzcka did was very similar to what I had seen animals do and it occurred to me it was this practice that made women have babies.

Thinking about what I had learned, I began to observe people in a new light. There was a learned man in Zyndranowa who had four very pretty daughters. They were too young to be married, yet each had several suitors already to choose from when the proper time should arrive. Then there was another man with four daughters long since past the marriageable age. They were so ugly no man would look at them. The father was a sort of bully and chased after women. This family was known to sleep in the same bed and every one of the four daughters had a baby. Of course there was some gossip. But no one got too upset, as illegitimacy among the peasants was common and quite acceptable.

Very soon I noticed the biggest and strongest men in the village were the ones with claim to the most women. Such a strong man would visit even a married woman at night. The husband knew about it. The whole village knew what was going on. But no one said a word, because if someone said something the strong man didn't like, the strong man would pay that person a visit. And no one wanted to get beat up or have their house wrecked.

Usually, the husband was afraid of the tough guy and did nothing about his wife's unfaithfulness. But this was not always the case. One day, I noticed the police were at the farm next door to grandfather Isak's. They were going in and out of the barn. I walked to the edge of grandfather's property. The door of the neighbor's barn was open and lying on the ground inside was the body of a peasant who was a friend of Mordecai and known to be a very tough man. When he saw a woman he wanted, he went right after her whether she was married or not. It was widely known he was paying visits to the neighbor's wife. Now the man's head was in two pieces and a bloody axe was near his body. The death of a Pole would normally have meant little to me because they often hated Jews for no reason. But this man was a friend of Mordecai, and the same kind of man as Mordecai. I thought of Mordecai lying there on the barn floor and the vision made me tremble with fear for the life of my uncle.

* * * * *

It seemed I was at grandfather Isak's farm barely long enough to shake off the dust of Bielanka when it was time to go to Dukla and resume *Cheder*. By this time I was becoming used to change: living here, living there, visiting the homes of strangers and getting for myself what I needed. Very easily I could have hitchhiked back and forth to Dukla. But once again I stayed at the home of Mr. Hershel. When my father came to Dukla to pay for my lodging I generally avoided him.

During this time Faye was also in Dukla, a little Jewish *shtetl* near the Czechoslovakian border, studying to be a nurse, but seldom did I run into her. Mr. Hershel rarely came out of his room, and when I wasn't at *Cheder* or having dinner at the home of some Jewish family, the house was mine to do with as I pleased.

Dukla was where I happened to be when the Germans marched on Poland. The Polish radio blasted away: "We shall defend our land. We'll defeat the German armies. We will not give up even a button of our coat." Such words meant far more to me than the German threat. The Polish armies were passing through Dukla towards the Czechoslovakian border and I felt certain the country was secure. But soon enough, there were sirens and gun blasts and bombardments and low-flying planes and retreating Polish armies and us staying in the darkness of cellars. During the afternoon German planes machine-gunned Dukla and the retreating Polish units. From the city hall building Polish soldiers fired their handguns at the terrible German flying machines. The firing of guns shook the ground. The cellar I was hiding in was packed with trembling people, and cries and sobbings filled the darkness. About two weeks after the war started the firing stopped. The streets of Dukla, built for the horse and cart, vibrated with the weight and roar of German army trucks and tanks.

Dukla was famous for its gap, which led through the Carpathians to Czechoslovakia. I looked through the cellar window that faced the market place. The Germans were marching right through the Dukla Gap, and it seemed there were one hundred thousand of them. Poles were standing along the edge of the road waving to the passing cars, military trucks, and motorbikes. I climbed up out of the cellar and the Germans came marching like the links of a never-ending chain. From the marching column rose the odor of leather, cloth and oiled metal. This was the smell of cleanliness and efficiency and it was so unlike any of the smells I was used to, I thought the Germans inhuman. They didn't smell like real people. They didn't walk like real people. Their faces were all the same — hard and expressionless — and I couldn't tell one German from another. A German officer said something to a Pole who had evidently stepped too far out into the road. When these inhumans spoke the very breath that carried the word was a command. There was not the slightest doubt as to the punishment for disobedience, and the Pole jumped back for dear life.

For two days the Germans marched through Dukla, and then a strange and frightful thing happened. The German army had required food and, quite naturally, a shortage developed. Someone began a rumor the Jews were stockpiling food in their homes and shops. The Poles had to go hungry; but, according to the rumor, the Jews had all they could possibly want to eat. A few of the bolder peasants began going around to Jewish houses, knocking on doors and saying, "Hey Jew, give us some bread. We need salt. Hey, give us potatoes and candles." The Jews kept their doors locked. They were all too familiar with tales of the open door which led to robbery, rape and murder. The presence of a gentile defiled the home of a Jew, and no good was certain to come of it.

Then another rumor circulated: the Jews were having a big party at the other end of town, stuffing themselves with food while Polish peasant babies starved to death in the street.

As if this rumor were't bad enough, someone added to it the Jews had a Polish girl at this party and were raping her. It was at this point the Germans supposedly authorized all Jewish shops to be cleared of merchandise.

I had just finished dinner in the home of a Jewish family when the trouble started. The door was locked. We huddled together fearfully as it shook under the impact of some sort of battering ram. We knew of the rumors circulating among the Poles. For dinner, we'd had a very thin soup, but the Poles wouldn't have believed us had we been brave enough to tell them. They were convinced we were holding out on them. This was what they wanted to believe and nothing would change their minds. The door shuddered on its hinges and we looked at each other as if for the last time.

Then there were cries outside, shouts and screams. The pounding on the door stopped. After a few moments of fearful waiting, I ran to the window and looked out. Across the street the Poles had broken down the door of a Jewish home. Polish peasants I had met and often talked to were running out of the house with linen, food and cooking utensils. On their faces were mixed expressions of joy, horror, and frenzy that sent absolute chills down my back and belly. Never before had I seen such expressions, and they made the people who had them seem like total strangers. One Pole came from the house dragging a young girl, struggling, biting and scratching. The Pole threw her to some other Poles and they ripped the clothes from her body. In full view of hundreds of people, seven Poles raped her, one after the other. Some members of the Polish intelligentsia of Dukla looked on indifferently. The Germans who pushed their way through the crowd seemed amused.

From the girl's house ran her brother, and he leaped on one of the Poles who had raped his sister. At this the Germans were not amused. A soldier in officer's uniform stepped forward and pistol-whipped the Jew. Then he stepped back and some other soldiers came forward and kicked the Jew before dragging him to his house and throwing him inside.

The Poles, both peasant folk and townspeople, continued to loot Jewish homes and businesses, and beat up the Jews they managed to get their hands on. After several hours the Germans dispersed the mob. By the following day the Poles had lost their expression of frenzy. They greeted the Jews in a friendly manner, as if nothing at all had happened.

* * * * *

The enemy occupation of Dukla happened so fast it was like falling off a cart and waking up in a strange house. The town looked as if it had been hit by a hurricane. Roofs were missing from houses, holes dug in the streets and windows smashed. Bodies lay for hours along the roads. Polish soldiers and snipers lay dead. So did innocent peasants and peaceful Jewish merchants. As the enemy marched through the town some of the soldiers were making a house to house search for snipers. From a broken window I watched a pair of Germans coming down the street. They kicked open doors and stepped inside, pointing their rifles. I thought how terrible it would be to be a sniper and have those big, machine-smelling Germans kick open the door. Never had I seen such a methodical search and I thought, "These Germans know what they are looking for." The thought chilled me, and my heart beat to bursting even though I didn't think I had anything to fear.

The soldiers reached the house across the street from where I was hiding behind the broken window. The cobblestones of the street were torn up and scattered about, and one of the Germans stood next to the door while the other kicked it open. In front of the building was a large window which had somehow escaped being broken, and through this window I saw them approach the occupant, who was a Jew with a long dark beard. The man's jacket was also dark and his shoulders were slightly stooped. His hand was trembling by the corner of his mouth and the look he gave the Germans was full of fear. One of the soldiers stepped up to the man and took hold of his beard. All the way across the street came the voice of the German: "Swine! Jewish dog!" and still holding onto the man's beard, the German hit him in the face with his pistol.

Through the window the blood on the Jew's face was clearly visible. A woman rushed into sight from a back room of the building. She flung her stout body at the German and I could hear her cries for mercy. The German led the Jewish man about by the beard and dumped him on the floor. The second German, who had been watching and laughing all this time, stepped forward and grabbed the woman. She tried to stoop and tend to the fallen man, but the German yanked her to her feet. Then he spun her around and with one jerk pulled off her clothes. I couldn't believe my eyes. From my post at the window I watched the German throw the woman on top of the man on the floor. The Germans were both laughing.

My grandmother came from Zyndranowa to fetch me. She had heard that many people were shot during the invasion. To Dukla she came in fear some German would not like my face.

32

A SAMPSON CALLED BERGMANN

Before I even got off the wagon, Faye came flying out of the farmhouse. She threw her arms around me and cried, hugging me and sobbing as if she hadn't seen me for ten years. Just before the war started, she had left Dukla. News of the German invasion had spread quickly and she no doubt thought me lucky to be alive.

"Have you heard from Daddy?" she said.

"No. I guess he's in Bielanka with his new wife."

She frowned at me. Still sparkling in her eyes were the tears of our meeting.

She said, "Moishe is with him. Yes, they must be in Bielanka. But I wish they would visit us. The Germans are killing a lot of people and it seems they don't like Jews. I don't know what we have ever done to them. But it seems they don't like us and I am afraid for Moishe. Oh Shmulek, I'm so glad to see you!" She threw her arms around me and cried some more. "I am afraid and don't know why. I wish Daddy were here."

Mendel came up behind us. He put his arm around Faye and held her to his shoulder. "Everything is all right," he said. "We will take care of you. Shmulek is all right, as you can see. And so is Moishe and your father. If any Germans show their faces around here we'll chase them off."

Faye dried her eyes and smiled weakly. Mordecai walked around the corner of the barn and Faye looked in his direction. Mendel dropped his arm from her shoulder and got an expression on his face as if he were mad at something. Grandmother had gotten off the wagon and gone into the house. I waved to Mordecai and took off after her, hoping to find an extra piece of pie or buttered bread.

The German invasion of Dukla had certainly been a terrible thing. A town had been devastated, its people sent crawling into dark places. But the farm in Zyndranowa was isolated from all that. The house of my grandfather seemed far away from the Gestapo patrols, and farmwork continued pretty much as usual.

Part of my job was caring for the horses and cattle. This I liked very much. There was no school, nothing to learn. Farm life was grand, with plenty of homemade food. My grandparents were wonderful to me, even though they didn't speak to each other. My uncles were very kind and both of them were great fun to be with. In short, it was paradise to be away from the Germans, and away from the city of Dukla, which had become a city of hunger and death. The mornings were sunny and bright, the air filled with the rich wonderful smells of farm animals. The earth was free to walk on and the people around me I loved.

One morning a cloud blotted out the sun. The village of Zyndranowa was Ruthanian, and the Nazis asked the Ruthanians where the houses of Jews were located. The villagers were only too glad to give such useful information, and five Gestapo men pulled up in their car in front of my grandfather's house.

The face of my grandfather turned suddenly white and ghostly. Everyone was in the house except Faye, who for some reason was not. The Gestapo was known to tell young men to report to Gestapo headquarters from where they would be sent to a work camp or a concentration camp; so my uncles cleared out of the house. We made sure everything was in order and that the dog was out of the way (they sometimes shot dogs that dared bark at them). I went out the back door of the house to chase the chickens away, for if the Germans saw a chicken they might demand its head be cut off. Sometimes they had chicken and other meat delivered to their headquarters.

As I rounded up the chickens and chased them into the orchard, I heard the car doors slam. My heart nearly burst through the skin of my chest. Peeking around the corner of the house, I saw the driver had remained in the car. The others went to the door and my grandfather opened it. The soldier in front, who must have been the leader, said, "Are you a Jew?" My grandfather answered in Yiddish, his voice trembling, "Yes," and the four Germans walked into the house as if they owned it.

The door shut. I felt my place was with my grandparents and I ran around the house and in through the back door of the kitchen. The Gestapo leader glanced at me and said, "Where is the rest of your family?" My grandparents stood together in front of the stove. "Where is the rest of your family! Can't you hear?"

"I don't know," said grandmother.

The officer looked at her, his eyes hard and full of mischief. The other soldiers looked around the house, as if they were calculating the value of the curtains and furniture. Maybe they thought money was stuck under the chairs.

"Does the woman wear the tongue for her man?" said the officer. "That is not the way we Germans are. I can see very plainly why you Jews are such a weak and miserable race."

"I don't know where the rest of my family is," said my grandfather.

"Ahh, now the man has a tongue!" The German walked over to my grandfather and pushed him gently back against the hot stove. Isak didn't dare resist. "Did you know there are three Jewish families living in this filthy village Zyndranowa?"

"Of course," said my grandfather, his face white as wax.

"Respect! You will speak to me with respect!" The officer pushed against my grandfather's chest a little harder. The smell of singed cloth was filling the kitchen. "Are you also aware you are considered the wealthiest?"

"I am but a poor man," said my grandfather. "Each day I work hard and for very little more than the food in our bellies."

"I want your gold."

My grandfather answered politely in Yiddish, "Sir, I have no gold or diamonds. I am but a poor man."

"I didn't ask for diamonds, did I? Where are they?"

The officer waited a second, then stepped back. One of the other soldiers stepped forward and knocked my grandfather down with a slap on the face. Then he turned to my grandmother and laughed fiendishly. Reisel turned her face toward the man on the floor and for the first time in my life I saw her look upon her husband with despair and great pity.

The Gestapo brutality had been horrible to witness; but it was the look my grandmother gave her husband that struck horror in me. I tried to run out of the house but one of the Gestapo men grabbed me around the waist and threw me in the opposite direction. My grandfather got up off the floor and Reisel steadied him by holding his arm. We backed into a corner. The officer unsnapped his holster and took out his pistol. The other soldiers leveled their rifles at us. With their thumbs they moved certain attachments of the rifles and the clicking noises raised the hair along the back of my neck. In that moment, when I was certain I was going to die, my mind played a trick on me. I remembered an incident involving a Polish boy.

Now the Poles were very superstitious. They not only believed in ghosts, but also believed there were specific places haunted by ghosts and all manner of frightful things. Well, there was this one boy some other peasants played a trick on. They told him there was a haunted place and made a bet he was afraid to spend the night there. He said no one would do such a thing; so the other boys all stayed there overnight to prove they were brave. This boy now had to show he wasn't a coward and he stayed overnight at the haunted place all alone. During the night the other boys played a trick on him, and it wasn't long before everyone was horrified to find that his hair had turned white.

This is what I thought about as the officer raised his pistol and pointed it at my grandfather's face. I thought about my own hair and how white it must be at that moment.

"I will ask only once more for your valuables."

I started crying and my grandparents begged him to let us live. As I cried, my mind seemed detached from my body, as if it belonged to someone else. I thought how stupid it was to cry when the next minute I would be dead. Nothing seemed to matter. Certainly not tears. Yet I couldn't catch my breath. My body quivered and shook and there was a steady whining sound I recognized as my own. My grandfather was down on his knees begging for the lives of his grandchildren, his children, his wife. The German officer just stood there, expressionless, his face strong and powerful and hard as rock.

Suddenly outside was a scream. The Gestapo man dropped his arm and he and his men rushed out the door. I staggered to the window. Outside, the Gestapo man who had driven the car was kissing Faye. She was pinned against the car by the man's fat arms and her face was twisted with terror. Her shoulders were bare and it looked like the German was biting her on the neck.

The officer shouted at the driver and he released her. She ran away from him, but one of the other men ran after and caught her against the side of the barn. He could have broken her in half as easily as if she were a twig, and he said something in her ear while holding her against the barn. My grandparents were next to me at the window. They were both on their knees praying in a loud voice to God. The man holding Faye released her. Then the officer gave a signal and they all got into the car and drove off in a cloud of dust.

Faye came into the house with red eyes and tears on her cheeks. Everyone sobbed together, even grandfather Isak. Reisel rested her hand on her head. Faye said she had to report to the Gestapo station in Dukla. She didn't know why; no reason had been given. But no one refused a request of the Gestapo.

No one said much of anything. For a while we all sat around half dead; then my uncles came out from hiding. I guess they were outside someplace or in the attic. Faye really should have been with them. They, who had missed the horror, tried to restore some semblance of normalcy to a day we all wished had never come. We tried to eat but no one could get the food down. Someone told a funny joke. I didn't quite understand it, nor was I aware of who told it. But I did smile and it felt like a very strange thing on my face.

That night I slept very fitfully. The blankets were wet with perspiration. And in between cold sweats I had a dream. No longer was I a small boy. A weapon was in my hand and the Nazis were not so big and impervious anymore. They were mortal creatures with red blood like chickens and cattle. I dreamed I ordered these Nazis out of my country Poland, out of the house, and their cruel faces melted; because they were just mortal men.

The days that followed were quiet and desperate. Everyone knew what the other person was thinking: Faye might not return, she might be sent to a concentration camp or harmed in some way. Mendel looked like he would burst into tears at any moment. In fact, this is what he often did, and everyone else as well. Mordecai was the most reserved of anyone. He came up with the suggestion Faye not report to the Gestapo station. Instead, he thought she should go to Bielanka and stay with father. My grandfather didn't think this was such a good idea. Both he and Reisel obviously disliked my father. Also, they were afraid the Gestapo might come back to the farm. For disobedience the Gestapo might shoot us all and burn the house as well.

"It is only the life of my niece I am concerned about," said Mordecai.

Grandfather Isak looked at his black sheep son. He put his hand on Mordecai's shoulder. "I have not always treated you fairly, but your heart speaks for all of us. I also am concerned for Faye. And I have other lives to think of also."

Mendel began to quiver.

"And why should you worry about Faye," he said to Mordecai. "Isn't it the other women of Zyndranowa you should be concerned about?"

"I merely suggest Faye not present herself to the Gestapo," muttered Mordecai, looking at her with sadness.

"Now is not the time to argue," said Isak.

Mendel's neck was red and he shouted:

"You want to be a tough man like Bergmann, is that it? Well, I can tell you Faye is not impressed. What is it that happened to Bergmann, hah — isn't he dead? Yes, this big tough man was no match for German bullets and for all his bravery he is now dead. His very own family can no longer count on his protection and it is his mother and his sister the Germans visit. Oh yes, you think I haven't heard? They visit them by the carload!"

"That has nothing to do with Faye. As for Bergmann, you have no right to say such things of him. Who was it who made the Poles respect the Jews on market day? Bergmann. When the Poles would have got drunk on Jewish whiskey and then beat up the Jews who served it to them, there was Bergmann to make the Poles change their mind. Sure Bergmann was tough. He was a good fighter. And when he was around the peasants didn't drive through mud puddles in order to splash some Jew. He was certainly no coward. And when the Poles were raping his sister he wasn't one to stand by and let it happen."

"He was a scoundrel. A woman-chaser. He slept with other men's wives."

"If you had only a little of his courage you wouldn't be saying such things."

The brothers glared at each other. In the brief silence I recalled this man Bergmann. One time he was on the road from Dukla to Zyndranowa and I asked him for a ride. As we jolted along on the cart, Bergmann spotted a peasant girl walking along the road and stopped the horse alongside her. He told me to climb into the back of the cart and the peasant girl took my seat. Immediately, he started to kiss her and squeeze and pinch her. He turned around and winked at me, as if to say I shouldn't look on. His look said: "Look, boy, you're too young. Just go to sleep in the hay."

There was another Jewish fighter-type, also, who was Bergmann's friend. As long as the two of them were around, the Jewish merchants weren't afraid of the Polish peasants or town dwellers on market day. They were the community's overseers, champions of justice and Jewish rights.

Oh . . . how we needed Bergmann and his friend now! Why can't all Jews be like Bergmann — unafraid, tough, who could smash anti-Semitic heads? Why are our heroes the rabbis, the scholars, the Talmudists, I thought to myself? My stream of

36

thoughts would not leave my hero Bergmann. I remembered one summer market day (*Yerood*) in Dukla, where hundreds of peasants gathered once a week to trade, barter, and sell their crafts, cattle, sheep, horses, butter, fresh fruits, etc. The town's market place was literally crowded with people and animals. There were noises, haggling, and eternally violence and abuses. Suddenly, as I sat at the north corner of the market place, a stirring of crowds and loud noises and screams followed. It was five drunken peasants trying to steal some cloth from a Jewish pushcart peddler. Like Superman, on the scene appears Bergmann and a friend who was a baker by trade. Some fierce punches were thrown at the peasants and all five of them were bleeding on the cobblestones. Shortly thereafter the Polish police arrived and though usually anti-Semitic they wouldn't argue with Bergmann and friend. The peasants were arrested by the Polish police and the proceedings on the market place continued until sundown. This Samson of Dukla was looked down upon by the "proper" Jews, who felt that Bergmann and friend were *apikorsim* (non-observing Jews) who didn't keep the Sabbath and even rode horse and buggy through the town on the holy day. Yet this non-observing Jew defended the weak and the feebleminded. Polish anti-Semites used to enjoy taunting the town's feebleminded, the idiots, and the beggars, of whom there were plenty in the *shtetl* of Dukla. Bergmann and friend made sure that the same ignorant Polish anti-Semites would not do this taunting twice. Oh, how I wished that we had a million Bergmanns now who would rid us of the German occupiers of our Polish soil. But it was an empty daydream and my attention latched back onto the arguing brothers.

This argument between brothers I didn't like. I couldn't understand why Mendel was so angry at Mordecai. Mendel's cheeks were red and his now clean shaven face sparkled with perspiration. He glared at Mordecai and ground his teeth together.

"You are not so tough as you − − −"

"Mendel!" said grandmother. "Enough! I will not have my sons fighting at a time like this. One is never too old to show respect in his father's house."

Mendel stormed from the house slamming the door behind him. Mordecai sat down at the kitchen table. He covered his face with his hands. After a moment he made two fists and brought them down hard on the tabletop.

My grandparents decided Faye should report to the Gestapo as ordered. They also decided I should be the one to drive her because I looked pretty much like a gentile boy and it was less dangerous for me to be seen on the streets of Dukla than either one of my uncles.

The following morning Mordecai hitched up the horse. He kept his eyes on the ground and said very little. Faye and I climbed up onto the wagon seat and off we went. From Zyndranowa to Dukla was a distance of about twenty miles. Normally, having the reins in my hands would have made me feel so important I would have enjoyed every second of the journey. It was men who drove the horses and seldom did I get the chance. On the few occasions I was in the driving seat, I felt I was doing a manly thing in spite of my father's lack of confidence in me.

But under these circumstances it wasn't very exciting at all. I was afraid of what the Gestapo were going to do to Faye and the kilometers seemed to pass all too quickly. Every now and then Faye tried to say something funny, just to see me smile. The road was poor with ruts and deep holes. The terrain was rocky and below the road was a river.

Shortly after noontime we arrived in Dukla. I left the horse and cart on a side street and we walked to the Gestapo headquarters, which was in what had been the Polish mayor's residence before the war. As we approached the guard Faye's steps slowed down and her knees shook. The guard asked what we wanted. Faye said she had been asked to report to a man named Finke. I was kind of surprised to hear the name spoken aloud. For some reason it had not occurred to me the Gestapo would have human names.

The guard told us to wait in the corridor of the huge building. Soon Herr Finke came out. He seemed both surprised and delighted we had come. Apparently he did not remember making the request. Faye told him I was her younger brother.

* * * * *

Finke was a gigantic man with red face and clipped blond mustache that didn't move when he talked. The guard left us and we were told to come into a reception room. It was a cold, white room with a picture of Hitler hanging on the wall. There was the fantastical aroma of cigar smoke. Finke closed the door behind us and then, surprisingly enough, spoke to me in a friendly manner. His words were Polish which I understood very well. Faye was white and I could smell her perspiration. Finke said I should not be afraid and offered me some sweets. I thought perhaps they were poisoned, but I did take them for I imagined he would kill me if I didn't.

He asked how we had made the journey and I said by horse and cart. He seemed amused that we had come all the way from Zyndranowa. Then he called down the corridor. I thought, "Now the other four will come. All five of the men who came to the farm will be in this room and what will happen to us then?" The person who came was the guard who had seen us into the building. Finke told him to see me outside so that I could look after the horse and make certain it wasn't "stolen." I asked in Polish, "What about my sister?" He said she would come along after they had had a little talk. Faye smiled, as if to say, "Everything will be O.K.," and the guard escorted me to the door.

While waiting with the horse, I imagined all the horrible things that could possibly happen to Faye. What would I say to my grandparents if I couldn't take care of her? What was love if I couldn't even take care of my sister? I felt pretty foolish, then, because the whole trip to Dukla had been unnecessary. Finke didn't remember telling Faye to report to the station. We had all been worried sick and my grandparents were afraid of losing the farm. Mendel and Mordecai had nearly come to blows; and Faye and I walked into the jaws of the lion, like two dumb rabbits.

Now we had every reason to be afraid. We were in Dukla with the Gestapo, and I stayed with the horse for what must have been nearly an hour, shaking with fear. I started walking around in circles and jumping on the spot to keep warm. Then I decided to walk back to the Gestapo headquarters. Perhaps Faye was on her way to meet me. It was only a ten minute walk from the horse and cart. The town clock struck three. I did not know what to do. Timidly, I walked sticking close to the buildings. Some Jewish men passed me with their shaven beards and sorrowful eyes. All Jews had to shave off their beards as soon as the Germans occupied Poland. As I neared the Gestapo headquarters, Faye came out of the building and walked down the steps to the sidewalk. My heart beat suddenly faster. She walked all right, I thought. She looked O.K. She didn't look beat up or anything; but she was crying and looked worried. I reached her out of breath and asked what the matter was and she answered in a tone that said she was going to cry harder: "Nothing!"

38

We started off for home, whipping the horse to a fast trot. Faye looked upset and I asked her whether Finke had beat her. She said no. By the time we arrived in Zyndranowa it was late and very dark. As we approached the farm I could see lantern light in the window and the whole family waiting. Grandmother came running out on the porch. "It's the children. It's the children. Thank God, the children are back."

Uncle Mordecai took care of the horse and we went into the house. Supper was waiting and I was cold and starving. Faye couldn't eat. Grandfather asked her what the Gestapo wanted. "Nothing," she said, bursting into tears and running from the kitchen. Reisel looked at me and asked me what had happened. I said I didn't know and she got up from the table and went after Faye.

After dinner I fell into bed and didn't move all night long.

The next day I overheard grandmother saying to Mordecai that Herr Finke and the others at the Gestapo station had made advances on Faye and that she was very much afraid Faye had been raped. Then I realized why Faye had been so melancholy during the trip home from Dukla. At breakfast she ate a little and after we finished I offered to help her with the dishes. I felt sorry for her and wanted to make her laugh. I tried to tell something funny but it didn't work. She didn't talk much. Finally, I did manage to make her smile.

The weeks rolled by and then father came from Bielanka to see Faye and me. Curiously enough, I was happy to see him. By horse and cart he came and I noticed he didn't look well. He looked skinny. Most shocking of all, his beard was shaved and his naked face looked weak and sickly. Breathlessly I asked, "Are you O.K.?"

We embraced and his face said, "Yes, son." Never had I felt so close to him. The brute of a man the peasants left alone because he was big and strong; the good *soicher,* educated in the Torah and Jewish tradition, who knew nothing of the religion of his Christian neighbors; the man I at times hated because he treated me like a child. He smiled and I felt warm all over. The look he gave me was the look adults give someone they love. I liked it when he called me "son," because it made me feel like he thought about me.

"What happened to your beard?"

His eyes were deep and tired and I thought at first no words would pass his lips on this matter. Then he spoke slowly looking over the top of my head at the fields and houses in back of grandfather Isak's farm.

"Long ago, the Jew was invited to this land by the Polish kings to help improve the land. It was a great honor, and to this day, certain Jews wear strange clothing. On high holidays they wore fur hats and long *kapotas* and white stockings which are copies of medieval nobility."

He stopped talking and I waited with downcast eyes. He was merely telling me what every Jewish boy learned from the stories of the *melamed.* Yes, the Jew was invited to Poland and he prospered, as did the gentile Poles. So what my father said came as no surprise to me. What was touching was that he chose to speak at all to me, the son he had never seemed to trust. I waited, thinking perhaps he would say no more.

"There is much that has always belonged to the Jew. His way of living . . . ."

Once more I waited and waiting was agony.

"In a *shtetl* not too far from here called Zmigrut, a man had a very lovely, long and well-cultivated beard. He was a rabbi, a widely known and very respected man. One day the Germans drove through his *shtetl* on their jeeps, and most of the Jews ran to their houses and bolted the doors and hid. This rabbi refused to run. The Germans could tell he was a Jew because of his beard. So they jumped out of the jeep and grabbed him. They tied his beard to the bumper and drove back and forth across the marketplace until he died."

As he finished speaking I could feel his eyes upon me. I was trembling and unable to meet his gaze. (Later, we heard of several similar stories.)

"I am no less of a Jew," he said, "because I choose not to wear a beard."

My grandfather came from the house and gave my father a rather perfunctory greeting. I was shaking all over and glad Isak had stepped in. Never had I thought of my father as a Jew; he was always my father. Now the events had pointed him out as different and inferior. Faye appeared while the two men were standing together exchanging what appeared to be grunts and nods. She ran to him, throwing out her arms: "I'm so glad to see you, Daddy!" He kissed her and they both went for a walk in the garden. Grandfather Isak shuffled off. His step was normally quite springy for an old man, but now he seemed heavy, as if he had left much unsaid while talking to my father.

When dinner was ready I went to find Faye and my father and caught up with them just as they were passing through the far end of the vegetable garden gate. They seemed happy. Faye was talking about the farm and father was telling her about Moishe and my stepmother and the new baby — our stepsister, Jaffa. Father took my hand in one of his and Faye's with the other. "You sure have grown up, son," he said with a smile. Faye said, "He should — he sure eats enough." As we walked along I pointed out to father the strip of grandfather's land. Of course, he already knew what grandfather owned; but in the quiet glow of good feeling that filled my body it was nice to be able to show him something as one man to another. Faye asked when he was going home. He said, "Tomorrow. I can't keep those at home wondering what's happening to me these days."

Suddenly, a strange yearning came over me. I hadn't seen my stepmother, Ester, in a long time. The thought of a new baby was exciting. The last time I had been in Bielanka was late in '37 or early '38, and I hadn't seen Moishe in a long time, either. The two days journey by horse and cart seemed like a great adventure. It would be great, a lot of fun, and I'd get the chance to live someplace else for a while.

As we neared the house the smell of Reisel's cooking came to greet us. I said, "Dad, I want to go with you." Both he and Faye looked at me in surprise. Faye, in particular, was speechless. As glad as she was to see father, it would not have even occurred to her that she might go with him to Bielanka. Father shook his head cautiously. "O.K., son, if you'd like to come. Your stepmother will be very pleased to see you. But I warn you, the journey will be very tough."

"I've done it before."

Darkness was quickly falling. Dinner was not quite ready. My grandparents accepted the news of my departure quietly as if they had anticipated it all along. My father sat in a corner chatting with my grandfather while Faye and grandmother set the table. All of a sudden I didn't feel so good. No longer was I certain I wanted to leave this place. It was too late, I told myself, too late to change my mind; and I walked outside for some air.

The barn door was open and the yellow light of the lantern spilled out onto the ground. Inside the barn the peasant girl my grandparents hired for certain chores was finishing milking the cows. I walked inside the barn to watch her. She was wiping off the teat of my favorite cow. A morbid thought came to me that maybe this was the last time I would see this cow give milk. My favorite cow it was, and I was leaving her.

"I hear you're going with your father," said the milkmaid, smiling up at me with crooked teeth. The lantern light made her hair look thick and yellow like butter. Her skin looked soft, her eyes dark and friendly, as she waited for me to respond. And I thought, "Even she knows! How could she know when only a minute ago I told my grandparents?" I felt miserable, miserable! I had never experienced such a heaviness on my heart before. This would not be the first time I went to Bielanka with my father. Yet for some reason the decision felt like the kind whose consequences one must deal with for the rest of one's life. Not knowing why I felt that way made me all the more miserable. The weight of the decision was a heavy burden on my shoulders and I became depressed. To the milkmaid I silently nodded.

Faye came into the stable calling my name.

"Shmulek! Didn't you hear me calling you? Dinner is ready."

As we walked toward the house I felt a very strange sensation. It seemed I was as light as the wind and for some reason would be unable to enter the house; but rather I would blow right over it and out among the stars where there was only cold and loneliness forever.

"Shmulek, you're not paying attention to me. What's the matter? Don't you feel good?"

"No, I'm fine. Don't worry, I'm all right."

She said, "Tomorrow you're going with Daddy. I'm going to miss you, Fatty. You know it's just not going to be the same without you." I could say nothing; the words stuck like a ball of lead in my throat. We reached the veranda on the north side of the house. Faye took me by the shoulder and held me back.

"Promise me," she said. "Please, you must promise me you will never tell Daddy I went to see the Gestapo men in Dukla."

Looking at her sweet, gentle face, I almost broke out crying. Before my very eyes the face seemed to become that of a stranger. I wanted to throw my arms around her and squeeze and squeeze until something happened. Until what happened? I don't know. I was being silly. I told myself I was being silly.

"Don't worry, I'll never tell him."

She gave me a squeeze and went into the house. I followed. Everyone was sitting around the table and no one said a word. After dinner I went to bed. The night seemed to last forever. Every time I closed my eyes they seemed to pop back open. Finally, I got up and sat on the edge of the bed. There was my grandfather twisted in his blankets. My grandmother was a soft mound under hers. Faye lay with her head up, her face pale and beautiful. Mendel was snoring and Mordecai faced the wall. Each breath my father took seemed to shake the room.

Looking at each of these people I felt as if a cold knife blade were sticking in me and being twisted. I prayed to God to help me through the night. Then I sat on the edge of the bed until the rooster crowed.

The house was still dark and I tiptoed to the barn to see father's horse. The barn was warm with the smell of hay and manure. The horse stomped his hoof and made a low whinny and I rubbed his velvety soft nose. The journey would be tough for this gentle animal and I scratched his forehead and rubbed his neck. Then I went back into the house and lit the fire and woke up Faye. Silently I waited while she dressed watching her every move as if I were never to see her again. "You couldn't sleep?" she whispered, as we walked out into the kitchen.

"No. I guess I'm just too excited about the trip."

She tousled my hair. "Shmulek, how strange you are!"

She made breakfast and soon everyone was up and sitting around the table. Mendel made a joke or too but no one laughed. I couldn't eat anything.

"Look at Shmulek," said Mendel. "He must be sick, not eating anything."

"He's just excited about the trip," said Faye, smiling at me.

Grandmother seemed more quiet than anyone else.

After breakfast I went out with the men to harness the horse and make sure everything was all right. My father said goodbye to my grandparents and uncles. There seemed to be unusual warmth between them. Then he kissed Faye. I thought they were both going to cry. "You know you remind me more and more of your mother," he said. She smiled weakly. He hugged her once more, then jumped up on the wagon seat.

My grandmother Reisel kissed me and started crying.

"Will I ever see you again?" she said.

"Of course," I said, feeling like I was dying inside. "Why do you ask such a question?"

She said, "Promise me you will be a good boy and try to go to school so you will not grow up to be a *goy*."

I promised. I hugged her and kissed her and climbed up next to my father.

Faye shouted to us: "Maybe I will come and see you soon!"

And I smiled and nodded my head, waving, while tears ran down my cheeks. The morning was but a grey dawn and they stood all together in a group, first waving, then just standing watching me off, every now and then someone lifting a hand. It was when they were out of sight that I realized the wagon had been moving along the road. I turned around and the wind bit my wet face. My father pulled the wagon to a stop along the road.

"Here, why don't you take the reins?"

Without a word I took the reins, thinking, "Is this what it's like to be a man?" With a flick of the reins I started up the horse. The wagon bounced and shuddered along the rutted road. Father seemed to doze next to me on the seat. I looked to the horse, my friend.

We planned to spend the night at the house of my father's cousin who lived in Zmigrut. The horse was falling down as we approached the town. He was a nice speedy animal compared with grandfather Isak's old klunks. As a matter of fact, he had a tendency to run too fast, and horses of this nature are known to work themselves to death, said my father, who knew a lot about horses. He used to also be a horse trader before the war.

That night I slept very well at the home of my father's cousin, called Wolmut. We had a good breakfast which this cousin prepared. During the meal my father and Wolmut spoke of German brutality in Zmigrut. This I did not particularly want to hear. We had a lot of traveling to do and it was difficult making good time with a horse and wagon. As soon as breakfast was over we left Zmigrut and this time my father was driving. I had had my day behind the reins and I felt very good about it. My father turned onto a two lane road that was relatively smooth. I felt sleepy and he suggested I go to the back of the wagon where there was a little hay and sleep. This I was only too happy to do and the motion of the wagon rocked me to sleep.

The sound of a motorcar awakened me. I opened my eyes and was immediately blinded by the sun directly overhead. The hay made me sneeze. The sound of the motorcar got louder and I peeked over the side of the wagon. Coming down the road in a cloud of dust was a German car. My father quickly turned the horse to the side of the road, for the Germans always needed the whole road to themselves to speed through. The car was coming so quickly that my father didn't have time to quiet the horse. It reared up a little and he struggled with the reins.

The motorcar pulled to a stop in the middle of the road and dust drifted past the car. My heart was beating in my ears as I watched three Nazis get out of the car and walk over to my father.

One of them said, "Are you a Jew? Why isn't your *opaska* clearly visible? Are you hiding something, Jew?"

Without waiting for an answer he turned to one of his comrades and said, "You see? They shave off their beards and then think they won't be recognized." He turned back to my father and his eyes were blue and cold as ice. "They think we are stupid."

"Yes, I am a Jew."

One of the Germans looked over the wagon.

"Got anything in the cart?" he said.

"No. Nothing. I am just traveling to my home."

"I didn't ask where you were going. I said do you have anything in the cart. And that's all I said."

"No."

"You liar." The German stepped up to the wagon and slapped my father in the face. "Is the boy there 'nothing'? Maybe we will just shoot him then."

"Please, I want no trouble. Yes, I have my son in the wagon. Please do not hurt him."

The three men grinned and turned back to their car, laughing and barking to each other in German. The motorcar roared away and dust settled on the wagon. I crawled up to the wagon seat and asked my father if he was all right. He nodded, whipping up the horse.

"Did the slap hurt?"

"No. Go back and sleep in the hay."

"But I'm not tired."

"Do as I say."

Feeling hurt and rather foolish I crawled back to the hay. I lay down and closed my eyes. I kept thinking how unjust and humiliating it must be to be slapped for no reason. When I opened my eyes it was dark. The air was cool, the stars bright spots in the sky. The horse was standing still in the harness and father wasn't on the wagon seat. We were in Bielanka. My stepmother, Ester, came out of the house. With her was my brother Moishe. There was alot of tension in the air and no one seemed too excited about my arrival. I asked about the baby but she was asleep. And early the next morning, Moishe hitchhiked to Zyndranowa. He didn't like to live in Bielanka and wanted to return to see Faye and my grandfather Isak and grandmother Reisel.

As a boy of ten years of age, the seriousness of Hitler's plan for world conquest bothered me very little. Oh, I often heard my father say the Germans were killing innocent people. I myself had been with Faye in Dukla. I had been threatened by the Gestapo men on the farm in Zyndranowa and had seen my father get slapped in the face along the road to Bielanka.

But one could walk around Bielanka and not see German uniforms or hear the imperative German speech. In Bielanka the noonday sun shone warm on my neck and the people I met on the village roads smiled and said hello. It was a village of peaceful Ruthenians, where neighbors were still friends; and it was easy enough to forget the Germans were occupying our country.

My relationship with Ester had started on the wrong foot. The very first time I met her I had been frightened by her epileptic brother, and ever since then she looked at me with suspicion. Suspicion of what — I didn't know. I tried to be friends with her but nothing I did seemed to turn out right. The first child she had had with my father was a boy named Shaia. He was two years old, and I spent a lot of time with him. We became like buddies and even this Ester seemed to hold against me. I wanted to hitchhike back to Zyndranowa but the Germans had required that all Jews wear on their arm an *opaska,* which was the yellow Star of David, a symbol of disgrace and subhuman status.

"It is a long way to Zyndranowa," said my father. "And I will not allow Shmulek to go. With the *opaska* on his arm the journey would be dangerous."

"Why doesn't he just not wear the Star," said Ester. "He looks Aryan enough and no one will know the difference "

She looked at me and her eyes sent chills down my back. I wanted to shake her and say, "Why don't you like me!" But instead I felt cold and angry. I had very few good feelings toward her. My father looked at her and frowned.

"He is my son. He is a Jew. And he will not take such a dangerous journey."

I looked at my father with gratitude. He was a hard man and I was afraid of him. His own ethnic symbol he had shaved from his face; but it was no use. Anyone could tell he was Jewish in a Slavic country like Poland. It was my stepmother who got my father to shave. He called her a Delilah for it but at the same time was careful to keep his face smooth. Razor blades were becoming increasingly harder to find. It seemed many other Jews were shaving their beards, too, and among Jews, razor blades were sometimes used as currency, like money. One of my jobs was to get them for my father's use. To do this I traveled quite a bit in the immediate area around Bielanka.

Sometimes, just before the war broke out, I drove with my father to Bobowa, which was a small *shtetl,* about eighty percent Jewish. This was a delightful town. The buildings were kind of ramshackle and set on crooked streets of dirt and cobblestone. The streets were filled with bearded Jews and children playing. Dogs ran barking after wagon wheels and blue woodsmoke hung about the rooftops. Bobowa was a quiet place. A community of Jews who knew each other's names and looked after the welfare of all. On market day my father and I, as well as hundreds of peasants, drove to the marketplace and set up our booth of farm produce. There were booths selling anything imaginable: textiles, boots, tools, all kinds of wooden products made by the nearby village craftsmen, and all kinds of good food that filled the air with rich, delightful aromas. Horse traders were there with their horses; peasants that wanted to trade horses for cows, butchers that wanted to buy cattle for beef. Other livestock also waited to be sold. Some peasant would come up to a booth and haggle over the price. When he thought he had a good deal he would take the item. Sometimes he might think he was taken and this was when trouble was likely to start. The peasant might decide to get together with his friends and beat up the Jewish merchant. In Dukla there had been men like Bergmann to make sure this didn't happen. Bobowa had its strong men as well and my father was one of them. When the peasants saw his big chest and powerful arms they didn't think it was a good idea to cause any trouble.

All this was very exciting to me. For hours I would sit next to my father's booth or wander around the market place feeling glad to be alive. Sometimes my father would give me some money and I would buy ice cream (*loda*) and food and stuff myself. I liked to watch the pious Jews in the company of a rabbi walk around. They had strange looking hats and *kapotas* (coats). So slowly they walked! Their shoulders seemed bent with the weight of the world. Their brows were wrinkled with profound thoughts. The rabbi was the dispenser of justice, the chief judge and arbitrator, and his authority ranged from decisions as to whether the chicken was kosher to those concerning when the Messiah would come. My family observed Jewish ritual and tradition and expected me to do the same. But I could very easily appreciate the cynicism of a man like my uncle Mordecai.

Gradually a feeling of unrest crept up on me and my childish contentment seemed to grow more fragile every day. My father and stepmother were constantly on edge. The slightest thing would irritate them. The Jews I met on the street were no longer open and friendly. Haunted looks began to appear in their eyes. With tight lips and hunched shoulders they did their business, and market days lost their air of festivity.

A deliberate hatred of the Jews was being spread among the Polish people. This hatred was fostered by the Master Race and did not become serious until about 1941. We, the only Jewish family in Bielanka, were suddenly isolated from the other members of the village in which my father had lived in peace for a number of years. The Poles had always been suspicious of the Jews and may very well have hated them. The Jews regarded the Poles with contempt and caution, but we had still been on good terms. My peasant friends came to my father's home and enjoyed the homemade cakes of my stepmother and we got along fairly well. After the Master Race started its campaign my friends would still come over and enjoy Ester's baking, but they seldom talked. When they did their tone was filled with resentment for the occupying Germans. For Jews they had no love either. The poison and the anti-Jewish propaganda worked well.

One day a boy named Staszek said very suddenly: "Is it true that you Jews killed Christ our Lord?"

He was sitting in my father's house and his mouth was filled with my stepmother's baking. At first I didn't know what he could possibly have meant. But I soon found out the new village teacher had told the school children the Jewish race was the enemy of all people and that they had murdered Jesus Christ. Every day my father became more and more worried.

"Now the Nazis want young men to work in their labor camps," he said, pounding the table with his fist. "Where will it all end? It is not the Poles they want, either, but the Jewish men. First they beat us up. Stores are looted and girls raped. Then they say come and work in our labor camps, called *lagers* . Where will it end?"

The knowledge of Faye's experience in Dukla burned in my mind. I wondered how much father knew. When he said, "Some girls were raped," did he know that one of these girls was his own daughter? What would he do if he found out? He wouldn't hesitate to beat up a Pole, but I had never seen him so much as look defiantly at a German. And would he stand up to the mighty Gestapo?

How would I tell him in the first place? How could I tell him fear had made us stupid and we had walked right into the Gestapo station and offered ourselves up? The memory of what had happened made me sick with shame. More than anything at the moment, I wanted to go to Zyndranowa to see Faye. The faces of my grandparents, Isak and Reisel, beckoned to me. But here I was trapped in Bielanka.

Then my father, along with all other Polish citizens, received a new order from the Germans: all horses and cattle had to be registered with the German authorities. He planned to go to Mszanka and help his father, Herman Polster, register his animals.

"Why bother to do this?" said Ester. "Let's hide the animals for certainly we have need of them."

"Because . . . would you have me dead? The penalty for all disobedience is the same. The penalty for lying is death."

When he returned he reported that the city Jews were far worse off than those in villages. The German armies had used up all the available food. Rich Jews who lived in the cities had been reduced to beggars and poor Jews were starving in the streets. The Polish peasants were hungry, too, and blamed the Jews. Hardly a day passed that some Jew wasn't beaten up, robbed or killed and for this reason most of the Jews lived in houses shuttered and bolted tightly. A black market was flourishing alongside fear and violence.

About this time I decided to visit my grandfather Herman who lived in Mszanka. My father didn't have any objection to this, as Mszanka was only a short distance away — a few kilometers at the most. A Jew could still walk the streets of Bielanka in relative safety, and I should have no trouble crossing a few rivers and ridges that separated Bielanka from Mszanka.

Over the past few years I had made the trip to Mszanka several times and knew the road very well. With great joy I first caught sight of Herman Polster's farm. He had a small house of stone and wood, a barn, a woodshed and a chicken coop. Next to a garden was a cellar where he stored potatoes and milk. Ivy grew around the porch and excitement surged like electricity in my hand as I reached for the door knob. Behind me a cow mooed and I paused. I decided to savor that moment forever because it was filled with excitement, peace and tranquility.

When I saw Herman's face I was shocked at the lines of age in it. Of course, he was an old man. For over eighty years he had been on the earth. In this village, Mszanka, surrounded by the mountains, he had tended his land, cattle, two horses, goats and chickens. He was a small landowner who struggled each year to see his now small family and livestock through the winter. All his children except my father had left for America in the beginning of this century.

But it seemed that during the past few months he had aged at a rate faster than before. At one time he had been a robust man with wide apart blue eyes. Now those eyes were faded and watery. He suffered from asthma. His hair was white and feathery. In spite of these signs of age, however, his jaw was still firm. He still held onto the land.

My grandfather Herman's wife put her arms around me and kissed me fondly on the cheek. She was bovine-looking and rather unintelligent, but I liked her very much. Herman had married her when his first wife died. My father was a young boy at the time. By this second wife Herman had another son named Getzel. This boy was his mother's only son, her pride and joy, and hardly a day went by that she didn't take great pride in his accomplishments.

46

This kind woman always had something nice to say. In fact, she talked rather constantly and perhaps this was why Herman was often annoyed with her. She had some kind of permanent hernia. I could tell that because every time she sneezed some kind of black ring the size of a donut fell out from under her skirt. Frequently, he beat her. When I heard her cries I was sure to stay out of the way. On such occasions I was terrified. What a man did in his house was perhaps his own business. Unlike my grandparents in Zyndranowa, my grandparents in Mszanka at least spoke to each other.

On this particular trip to Mszanka I noticed right away the absence of Getzel. He was a lot like my uncle Mordecai. To me, at least, the absence of such men was as obvious as their presence.

"Where's Getzel?" I said to grandfather Herman. He looked at me in a strange way and his wife got red around the eyes and I knew right away I had said something wrong.

"He is in the jail in Gorlice, arrested for doings with the black market. You know what the black market is? He helped support us during these trying days," she added. Grandfather Herman squinted at me then raised his faded blue eyes to the hills outside the window of the house. "Then you know the Germans don't like it very much and even less do they like those who work with it. Getzel has become a criminal. Even worse, in the eyes of the Germans he was a Jew from birth."

"You mean they won't let him go?"

"Have you ever heard of a Jew being let go free by the Germans?"

My step-grandmother was howling in the bedroom. Herman shuffled off and I was left feeling there was no place on earth free of the German curse.

Sometime later my grandfather Herman asked me to go to the prison in Gorlice and take Getzel some food. My step-grandmother loaded boiled potatoes into a bucket. Underneath these potatoes she put some boiled chicken. It was strictly forbidden for the prisoners to have meat, so she hid the chicken well. Then off I went on the road to Gorlice.

Soon a cart came along with a peasant at the reins. He stopped and picked me up. We bounced and jolted along the rutted road in silence and I gripped the bucket between my legs as if it were treasure. Before long we passed some beggars on the road. With sad Jewish eyes they looked at us. One man supported himself with a stick. His coat was dirty and ragged.

"Hah! Some trick those Germans played on the Jewish dogs," said the peasant driving the cart. I looked at him with surprise thinking it strange he would talk like that to me, a Jewish boy. Then I realized I had not worn my *opaska*. Without the yellow Star of David on my arm there was no obvious way to tell I was a Jew and the driver had mistaken me for a peasant boy.

"Before the Germans came those very Jews along the road were fat with Polish wealth. They had done very well for themselves at the expense of the true citizens of this country. Now," he threw back his head and laughed, "They would give their coats for the potatoes in your bucket."

Fiercely I gripped the bucket as if the peasant might take it away from me.

"I have heard the Polish kings asked the Jews to live in Poland long, long ago."

The driver glared at me. "Who told you such nonsense? Say, are you a Jewish sympathizer?" He pulled up the horse. "Where are you taking those potatoes anyway?"

Fear closed like a fist on my throat. Every peasant in the country knew they could do nearly anything they wanted to a Jew and no punishment would be forthcoming. The Germans were entertained by Jewish misery. For their own safety Jews banded together, and here I was in the clutches of an angry peasant.

"To the Gorlice. To Gorlice!" I stammered. "My aunt lives there. She is ill and my mother sent me with some food."

The peasant continued to glare at me. Up and down he looked me over. Finally, he flicked the reins and the horse started down the road once more. The mood of the driver was soured and not another word did he say the entire way to Gorlice.

Inside the city I was only too glad to hop off the cart.

"Where's your aunt live?" growled the driver.

"Over there." I waved my hand in the general direction of the center of the city. Before the man could say anything else I took off, twisting through several streets until I was sure he could not possibly be following me. Pausing to catch my breath I felt the potatoes. They were stone cold.

As I walked along the streets of Gorlice I felt pretty good for having escaped from the peasant driver. After all, I had been in his clutches. He might very well have beaten me up. Not too long ago a Jewish boy in a similar situation had been maimed when the peasant drove over him with the wagon. So I felt pretty good and didn't even realize I was walking past the Gestapo station. For some reason I happened to look up — and there was a German standing on the balcony of the Gestapo station looking right at me. He waved and told me to come inside.

My knees nearly buckled as I climbed the steps. Over and over again I cursed myself, thinking how stupid I had been not to watch where I was going. Inside the door of the headquarters the German was waiting. Against his leg he beat a switch.

"When a boy walks past the station with a bucket of potatoes in his hand he is usually going to the prison," he said. "And those are potatoes, aren't they?"

"Yessir."

"And it just so happens that most people in the prison are Jewish."

Humbly, I mumbled, "Yessir."

"And are you Jewish?"

"I . . . ."

He slapped me and the next thing I knew I was lying on the floor looking at his black shiny boots.

"Why don't you wear the yellow badge on your arm as required?"

"I'm sorry. Really I am. I had no idea it wasn't on my arm."

"So. What are you carrying in the bucket?"

"Potatoes."

"I know that. What else do you have?"

"Nothing, sir. Nothing at all."

By now I was crying, choking with sobs. The German took the bucket and dumped it on me. Right there for all the world to see was the chicken.

"Nothing? Nothing else, you say? You know the rules, don't you? Take that! You filthy lying Jew! You know the prisoners aren't to have meat. Take that! And that!"

Again and again he kicked me. I rolled up into a ball and his boot struck my head, shoulders, belly, back and legs. "I'm sorry," I cried. "Please, oh please — I'm sorry — oh sorry — oh please!" He pulled my head back by the hair and kicked my face. Blood was on the floor from my nose, blood and potatoes and chicken. "Where did you get the meat?" he shouted. "I don't know." He kicked me again. "Where?" And again. "I don't know, I don't know!"

"Pick up this garbage," he said.

Blinded by tears and blood I scraped up the potatoes and chicken and put them back in the bucket. The German yanked the bucket from my hands and dumped it in a waste can. Then he threw the empty tin at my face. I ducked and he kicked me in the belly.

"If I ever catch you again without your armband, your *opaska*, I will kill you. Do you understand? If ever I catch you. And be certain I will keep my eyes open. Now get out of here. Get out!" He kicked me again and I stumbled out the door.

The next couple of days I spent in bed. When my body had healed I got a good scolding for getting caught by the Gestapo.

* * * * *

In spite of the tension of day-to-day living, my grandparents tried to make my stay in Mszanka pleasant. One Saturday morning I was given a new suit. With Jews all around us reduced to poverty and begging in the streets, this was indeed a very nice gift. Naturally, I should have gone to the *shul* in the next village of Moszczenica with my grandfather Herman.

Instead, I went out to the fields and ended up mildly taunting the cattle. Why I did such a thing I don't know. Perhaps I just felt so good I was bursting at the seams: such a mood lends itself well to taunting those stupid, lovable, bovine creatures.

Much to my horror one of the angry bullocks started chasing me. I fell in the mud and the bullock gored me a little, tearing my new suit. Needless to say, I had to go back to the house and explain how my suit got muddy and torn. I would have much rather grown wings and flown away. With each word of explanation I choked past my lips, grandfather Herman seemed to grow in size and terrible might. He was a tornado, a hurricane, the end of the world! But all he did was scold me to my pleasant surprise. As for the bullock, grandfather Herman sold it to some peasant and I never saw it again.

About this time the Germans ordered that no Jew was to move from where he lived. German patrols went through Mszanka and the terror of the cities spread to the country villages as well. Rumors were spreading that the Nazis were preparing ghettos for the Jews to live in. I had no idea what a ghetto was, but gone were the days when Hitler's plans meant little to me. The days of freedom through isolation were long past. I quite naturally assumed any plans the Germans had for the Jews couldn't be very pleasant and that it would just be a matter of time until I found out what a ghetto was.

The Nazis were diabolical creatures. They seemed to know the very thoughts in your head; and one day a Gestapo car drove up to the house of grandfather Herman. Five Nazis got out of the car. The leader did not look German. Rather, he had a touch of Slav-Ukranian in him, perhaps. He waited until Herman came out of the house. The other Nazis surrounded my grandfather. who obviously began to fear the worst.

"I hear, Jew, that you sold a cow."

The officer slapped Herman in the face.

"Is that true?"

"N-no. I w-would not do such a thing."

I stood there and watched my grandfather punched, kicked, and dragged in the mud. He cried and pleaded with them saying he was an old man and stubbornly denying he had sold the bullock. The Nazis beat this eighty-year-old man. They pushed his face in barnyard dung and made him eat it. And in spite of this, he refused to confess he'd sold the bullock. Whom he'd sold it to and where the money was hidden was a secret locked in his heart; and when the Nazis finally left he was a breath away from death.

My step-grandmother nursed him night and day until he was strong enough to get out of bed. The farm was falling into ruin. Herman had known exactly what to do and when to do it. Without him something always seemed to go wrong. The weeds choked the garden; the cows got into the grain; the horses refused to work. Night and day I prayed for his recovery; and it was a happy and thankful day when he appeared in the fields once more.

But he wasn't quite the same as he'd been before. The spring was gone from his step and he spent long moments standing still just staring at the mountains, breathing heavily. When he did that it gave me the chills for I was certain he was seeing something invisible to me. It wasn't long before he decided I should go back to Bielanka. "Life is too short," he said. "A boy must spend time with his family." Before I left he asked lengthy questions concerning Faye and Moishe and my grandparents in Zyndranowa. Thinking of these dear ones made me sad and I missed them terribly. Much rather would I have gone to Zyndranowa than to Bielanka.

Returning to my father's home did give me the opportunity to get to know my stepsister better. She was named Jaffa, after my mother, who had died of tuberculosis. Jaffa means "pretty" in Hebrew, and the child was well named.

As it turned out, I was to have a short stay in Bielanka. In June of 1942, Governor Hans Frank, the Nazi governor of occupied Poland, issued a proclamation that all people of the Jewish faith were to leave their homes and move to prescribed towns. Anyone of the Jewish faith not complying with the order within four days would be shot on the spot. The proclamation further stated that all personal property would be left behind except for bundles which could easily be carried. The town we were told to report to was Bobowa. This was to be our "ghetto."

My father and stepmother were deeply troubled. They walked around the house trying to figure out a way to carry along with us the most valuable articles and the most essential food, which was extremely scarce. Depressed and with a feeling of powerlessness, we climbed into a wagon provided by a kindly peasant neighbor. Each of us carrying as much as we could, we took a final look at our home where there had been a relative happiness and security. It was a simple house built after World War I. The roof was covered with tar paper like any number of Polish farmhouses; but it was ours, all ours. The harsh feelings my stepmother Ester and I had had toward each other now seemed like exchanges of love in a house full of life. I closed my eyes. Some Pole or Ruthenian would move into the ready-made comfort of a home. He would move into my father's house and defile it.

The horse was whipped a few times and started out fast. As the house disappeared into the distance, Ester broke into sobs. She must have felt it was the last time she would see her village. My father tried to console her saying the leave was temporary and that they would soon return. And perhaps she was convinced we would, in fact, return. Certainly I was convinced: for who could possibly have guessed the truth?

The first thing I noticed about Bobowa was that it had a barbed wire fence around some parts of it. This fence was entirely new and it struck terror to my soul. With pity in his eyes the kind peasant who had been my father's neighbor and who lent to us the use of his wagon said goodby to us. At the gate of Bobowa — a heavy gate of wood and barbed wire — he let us off and said goodbye for the last time. On the dusty street that used to enter a free and thriving *shtetl* before the war, my father stood holding in his arms all the bedding he could carry. Ester held the baby, Jaffa, and some food in a sack. I carried extra clothing and some more food; and my young stepbrother, Shaia, had in his little arms a potato for our dinner. We were not alone. All about us stood other people who held in their arms their earthly belongings. Not everyone in Bobowa *shtetl* had been Jewish. The Nazis had divided the town, and the Poles who now lived either outside the barbed wire enclosure or in special sections of the ghetto, gathered outside their houses and looked at us with curiosity. My family stood in confusion at the gate of the ghetto not knowing what to do next.

A greeting party of several individuals approached us from inside the ghetto. They walked with a peculiar heaviness, their eyes on the ground. One man detached himself from the rest and walked up to my father. He was beardless and rather skinny. I was shocked to see the emptiness of his eyes.

"I am a member of the *Judenrat*," he said. "The *Judenrat* is a council of Jewish elders, appointed by the Third Reich to take care of Jewish affairs here in Bobowa, as in other ghettos all over Poland. I will represent you to the *Judenrat* and pass on to you their instructions. Now I will show you to your new home."

No other words were spoken. I was bursting with questions and didn't really want to know the answers. Stumbling under the weight and bulkiness of our loads, we followed the member of the *Judenrat* down narrow streets and dingy alleys. The magic of Bobowa that I used to feel on market days before the war was now gone. The Germans had changed everything. In the manner of afterthought the member of the *Judenrat* turned around and asked our name. Apparently, this was an important procedure. The Germans had listed the names of all the local Jews, and anyone not showing up at the ghetto within the four day period set forth in the Proclamation would be considered a fugitive.

After my father stated his name the *Judenrat* member just stared at him in a rather stupefied fashion. He seemed to have a difficult time remembering everything he was supposed to do. He looked sick. As I learned later, the Nazis had been very smart: they avoided direct contact with the Jews by appointing the *Judenrat* council to look after the ghetto. This council was a mouthpiece for the Nazis, and the members of the council were sometimes rewarded for their cooperation with better living conditions.

But even the *Judenrat* was not exposed to the truth. They did as they were directed by the Nazis; but they, too, were Jews and lived in the same constant fear as everyone else. This man who was leading us to our new home stood in a state of confusion for a long time after the voice of my father had said our name. Then, he led us in a direction opposite to the one we had been traveling. Sometime after we were situated in the ghetto I was to learn that this man had shot himself. By then, death was such a common part of everyday life that the news neither shocked me nor caused any great concern.

* * * * *

Our house which consisted of one room was about twenty by eighteen feet. We found already living there my grandfather Herman Polster and his wife, as well as another family. My grandfather, also, had been brought there by peasants from Mszanka. The only furniture was a wooden table and some old and dirty straw mattresses thrown along the walls. The bathroom consisted of a smelly, wooden outhouse in back of the house which we shared with several other households. The room had no running water. The crowded conditions came as no surprise. In the Bobowa ghetto, literally hundreds of people were crowded into buildings that normally held about one-tenth that number. Each Jewish dwelling had a blue paint mark under its window so it could be distinguished from the gentile houses. Ester and my father piled our belongings on one of the mattresses. No one said much of anything. My step-grandmother gave us a sad look, as if to say: "I knew you would end up here. I was waiting."

"Where's Getzel?" I said, desperate to break up the tension of the room.

My step-grandmother burst into tears. Her eyes were red and swollen and I should have known she had been crying. And I should have known why.

"The Germans have taken from me my son," she sobbed, looking at Ester as if for pity. "From the prison he went to a concentration camp. There he developed a certain sickness. Oh, if they would only have sent him home to me! But no — what the Germans do is line up all the fine Jewish boys and send them to the right or the left. To the right would mean work in the munitions camp. To the left   . . . Oh, my son, I think they sent my son to the left. My only son . . ." She was in a hysterical state — mumbling away to herself.

Ester went to this woman and comforted her. My father stood in the middle of the floor staring at his feet, his face white as a sheet, his lips pale. At the wooden table sat Herman Polster. Completely expressionless, he stared at his sobbing wife. Like a dead man he looked, his face waxy and cold. My father walked to the table and sat down next to him. Neither one said a word or otherwise acknowledged the other's presence.

The night closed in steadily and a cold grey darkness filled the room. Ester spread our bedding on one of the mattresses and we got ready for bed. Along the far wall the other family who occupied the room did the same. The day had been one of the longest and most painful of our lives and we were tired to the bone. But no one slept. As I lay next to my stepmother, the coldness of the room seemed to take the breath from my body.

The woman of the family along the far wall was weak and sickly looking. She had not greeted us when we arrived. In the darkness of the night she was crying.

After what seemed like hours, Ester got up to see if the woman was in pain and I heard talk of a baby. The woman already had two children, about three and five years old, and I couldn't believe she was actually going to have another baby. I thought no man in his right mind would give his wife a baby at a time like this. Then I thought of my father and felt a twinge of guilt at being so judgmental, for my stepmother Ester was also pregnant for the third time.

My stepmother came over to our mattress and shook my father. He let her shake him a few times, then asked what she wanted. "A doctor," she said. "You must get a doctor."

"How am I to do that in the middle of the night? There might not be such a thing as a doctor in this place."

52

"You must go and see," said Ester, urgently. "Wake people up if you must. But hurry!"

My father got up and stomped out of the door. Ester then told me to wait outside. The children were asleep. Herman Polster seemed to have fallen into a coma. My step-grandmother was in pieces over the fate of her son, Getzel; but she rose from the mattress and went to help Ester. Stumbling about in the darkness, I left the room and stood shivering on the doorstep. The night was starless and damp. Off in the distance was the lonely bark of a dog, and I thought to myself: "A baby is actually coming into the world!"

After about an hour of shivering and waiting for the doctor, I heard the high-pitched cry. In a little while my stepmother came to the door and said I could come in. I followed her back into the house and found the woman's husband lying on the floor crying. The woman was asleep. The doctor arrived and the baby soon died. The doctor left. The baby lay in a corner covered with a rough blanket of some grey material. Herman Polster was muttering prayers and the sky outside the room's only window was the color of used wash water. The woman was still sleeping. Her husband left the room to see about the burial. My stepmother prepared breakfast for us and the woman's two small sons. Their mother was still sleeping and I felt sorry for them. Three weeks they had been in the ghetto. We ate some potatoes and a tiny piece of bread. Then my stepmother went to be with the other woman.

The baby's father returned with a crude wooden box. The baby had to be buried outside the ghetto. That day happened to be when the Nazis made one of their demands upon the Jews trapped in the Bobowa ghetto: all jewelry and other valuables had to be turned in to the *Judenrat*. Lack of cooperation would be punished by death. At the barbed wire ghetto gate, the Nazis examined the crude wooden coffin and its contents because there was a rumor the Jews were burying their gold.

Initially, the Bobowa ghetto consisted of a cross-section of the Jewish population. The young and old, the healthy and sick were all thrown together. Garbage and human waste piled up faster than it could be disposed of. Lice infested everything. Children walked naked through the cold damp alleys. Typhoid was common, as were diarrhea and dysentery. Jews who had once owned property and small businesses now dressed in rags. Elderly people, sickly and weak, supported themselves against the sides of buildings as they shuffled down the streets.

The most prevalent sickness of all was fear. What would the Germans do next? What was going to happen? At any moment the ghetto gate might swing open; German youths driving jeeps would careen down the narrow streets and alleys, purposely running down anyone in their path. For all their youth, these Germans were soldiers in the German army. They seemed to me only teenagers, yet they carried rifles on their shoulders; and when they got tired of chasing down pedestrians with the jeeps, they would yank those rifles off their shoulders and for the fun of it shoot down anyone within range. Laughing like school children, they would shoot out glass windows, and Jews packed like cattle into their houses had to take cover on their floors, with bullets and glass spraying over them.

There was no place to run from such abuse. The ghetto was like a box suspended in a den of wolves. Were a Jew caught outside the ghetto, the Pole who found him was handsomely rewarded. If the Polish policeman in the service of the Germans so desired, he could abuse the Jew with impunity before turning him or her over to the Gestapo.

Inside the ghetto, the *Judenrat* scurried everywhere trying to calm the people. They said the Germans were preparing a better life for us on the outside. They said the squalor of the ghetto was temporary. That someday we would be free.

The *Judenrat* said all young men were to report to the marketplace. The Nazis needed them for work in various camps. This was to be part of the new life. Any life seemed better than that in the ghetto, and the young men gladly walked to the marketplace, also known as the town's square, an area of cobblestones and trees, with buildings on four sides. The Nazis loaded them into military trucks and we never saw them again. We never heard from them again. The *Judenrat* said they were carving out a new life outside the ghetto and we believed because all we had was ignorance.

Then the Nazis wanted all men of particular trades. Once more the *Judenrat* offered us hope. "You see? These men will be working at jobs that will provide money for their families. Soon they will call for their families." And of course we all wanted to believe this. The Germans gave us a food ration but it wasn't enough to keep us healthy. The old and sick died off and the Germans cut back our rations, saying food should not be wasted on people not strong enough to survive anyway. Every spare piece of ground in the ghetto was used to grow vegetables. A couple of people even owned goats for milk to give their ailing infants. They had to be guarded intensely because they feared the goats would be stolen and butchered for food. There were rumors of cannibalism although I never knew firsthand of such a thing. People with bloated bellies walked around in a daze. Others died of starvation. Even our dead we could not protect from Nazi defilement, and the coffins were searched for jewelry.

So carpenters went to the marketplace. Tailors and shoemakers stepped up into the rear of military trucks, never to be heard of again. Little by little, men of health and strength were taken away. If ever the ghetto could have boasted a fighting force, that day was past and gone forever. A few relatively young men remained like my father and the man of the family we shared the room with. But they were not inclined to fight. For one thing, we didn't know what had happened to the men who had left the ghetto. For all we knew they may very well have been planning to contact their families. Certainly, it would have been unwise to provoke the Germans and cause our own death when salvation was possibly so near.

For another thing, a Jew was taught from birth to wait upon the rabbi, even as the rabbi waited upon the Lord. If there was a decision to be made of any importance at all, you went to the rabbi. He was a *hassid*, a pious man, and would intervene on behalf of his people. He knew what to do about everything, even Nazism, Germans and Hitler, and the persecution.

During the tragic moments in the Bobowa ghetto, the rabbis had one standard answer. All the rabbis I ever met or saw said the same thing: "Children, go and pray because the day will come when the Messiah will appear and he will protect us. The Lord knows what he is doing. He will help us." There wasn't one rabbi or other leader I know of who said to his people: "Children, let's take up arms. Let's train ourselves. Let's fight. Let's barricade ourselves and save our lives. Let's not obey the German laws any longer."

Life was torturous with anxiety and extremely dangerous. On Saturdays, the *Shabbat*, the day of rest and rejoicing, people were irritable, lonely, having nervous breakdowns and dying. The Germans took sport with our women. The heavy gate of wood and barbed wire swung open and the jeeps came through. One sight, in particular, filled me with horror. The Germans trapped a young girl in an alley. They pointed their guns at her and told her to undress. Then they made her get into the jeep and drove to the marketplace. There she was forced to dance for them. When the Germans tired of this amusement they tied her down and when they finished they left her there for the Jews to untie.

With lowered heads and haunted eyes the *Judenrat* passed on the news: the Germans wanted all women between the ages of fifteen and twenty-nine. Once more, the German military trucks came to the market place. When they left the heart of the Jewish people in the ghetto went with them. All that was left was a shell: the sick, the cripples, older folks and children. Old men muttered to themselves as they shuffled along the sides of buildings. Young mothers had remained in the ghetto with their babies, and the babies, weak and sickly as they were, sucked the life from their mothers' bodies. Garbage lay everywhere, sickness and death. The buildings were still overcrowded but now the wind roamed streets that seemed empty. People who happened to meet seldom spoke to each other. Long and hard they looked at each other and then passed on apparently not having seen.

The hollowness of these stares I couldn't stand. The spectre of death I saw everywhere made me want to scream, and I sought escape. I found there were places in the barbed wire fence surrounding the ghetto that I could squeeze through. For the first time in my life I appreciated the fact that I looked like a peasant boy. My blonde hair blended in with that of the gentile Poles and I roamed the countryside freely. At every opportunity I stole food and clothing, razor blades and candles. With these items I returned to the ghetto and my family was much better off than most of the other families. They had extra food and clothing. By the light of candles my father and grandfather Herman read the scriptures. Each day I risked my life to make things a little easier for them, and all I wanted in return was a little appreciation, a kind word or a gentle look.

However, this was denied me. My father rarely said anything and when Ester looked at me her eyes seemed dark and accusing. I thought she hated me for some reason. Everyone left in the ghetto lived in a state of fear and irritation and I was no exception. When I crawled through a hole in the barbed wire fence I left the ghetto behind, but I carried the fear with me. I carried with me the feeling I was hated by my stepmother. To a word one can respond, but how can one respond to a look? With bitterness I conjured her face in my imagination and stared back at her with hatred. With his silence my father abandoned me and I hated him for it, too. The one thought that gave me hope was that somewhere away from Bobowa was my grandfather Isak, my grandmother Reisel, the beautiful Faye, and Moishe, the only true brother I had. This thought I clung to. The Proclamation said all Jews had to report to ghettos and I had no reason to believe Isak and Reisel and my sister and brother had escaped this fate. But they were in a different part of Poland and had not reported to Bobowa. And since they weren't in Bobowa I didn't have proof of their imprisonment. I could believe what I wanted to and this was that they were free people waiting for me to be reunited with them. I simply would not believe they were suffering the same ignominy as my father and stepmother. To believe this would have given me all too little hope.

One day, while I was outside the ghetto, I met a Polish boy. He greeted me and I stopped dead in my tracks with fear. We were on the road leading out of Bobowa and a peasant drove his cart past us. The boy looked me up and down. He said, "Hey, who are you? I've never seen you before."

My heart was pounding so hard I thought I would choke. But I had to be brave! "Oh yeah? Well, I've never seen you before either."

"You talk a little funny. I'll bet you're a Jew."

"You talk funny, too. You're the one who's a Jew and maybe I'll turn you in to the Gestapo."

Just then a Gestapo car appeared down the road. I thought: 'Oh, no! Now I've done it! Now this stupid Polish kid will give me away and I'll be shot by the Gestapo.' The car drove on past us and the boy didn't make a motion to stop it. With great relief I watched the cloud of dust kicking up behind the shiny black car. The Polish boy looked me up and down again. I almost cried with joy when I realized all he wanted to do was fight. He squinted after the Gestapo car.

"You see those Germans? They have smiles on their faces. I'll bet they just came from some Jewish girl."

I realized a fight could probably be avoided if I showed this boy a lot of respect. But he didn't know anything I didn't know about women. If worse came to worst I was sure I could punch his stupid face in. Also, what he said about the Jewish girl made me both steaming mad and curious.

"What do you mean? All the Jewish girls are in the ghetto!"

"Goes to show what you know," said the boy, spitting in the dust. "The Jews are so dumb they do whatever the Germans want them to. First they send out all their men. Then all their money. Then all their girls. They're sure dumb. All the Germans have to do is ask and the Jews obey."

My knees felt weak. What did he know about the German "requests"? He had never been in the ghetto and had no idea what it meant to be offered a life outside the barbed wire. He had no idea what it was like for me to walk around the countryside like a free Pole, and then have to return to the barbed wire pen because that was where my family was kept like animals. For me to be caught outside the ghetto would mean instant death, and what did he know of endless fear?

I said hoarsely: "And what happened to these men who were taken out of the ghetto?"

Nonchalantly he shrugged. "Oh, I don't know. But I do know what happened to the girls." He sniggered. "Every single one of them are whores for the German army That's right! They do something to them so they can't have babies, then they send them to the fields. If they don't do a good job they get cremated. Three reports it takes and then a girl is turned to ashes. Ha-haw — "

In the middle of the third "ha" I hit him right in the mouth. I never had so much fun in all my life as beating the stuffing out of that stupid Pole. From my mouth came a hideous, insane noise; when I finished with him this noise turned to sobbing. The boy staggered to his feet and limped away. I screamed: "I am a Jew, you scum, you cow dung, you stupid — " Picking up stones, I ran after him hurling them at him and he ran shrieking down the road.

Then I stopped still and regained my composure. Fearing the boy would return with the Gestapo I worked my way back to the ghetto. My mind burned in agony, not for myself so much as for my father and Ester. Grandfather Herman was a man with one foot in the grave. He would accept rather stoically whatever was to happen. But my father still prayed every day for freedom. He said, "God will save us." He talked to the rabbis and believed the words of the *Judenrat*. And Ester, my stepmother, had two children to raise. Each day she prayed for their future giving no thought to herself. What would they say if they knew that our women between fifteen and twenty-nine had been released from the ghetto only to be field whores for the German armies? What kind of hope could they find in knowing that? How could I possibly tell them?

The day was Thursday. Distressed as I was, I remembered to take back with me the rabbit I had stolen from a Polish farm and put in a burlap sack. When I once more saw the faces of my family, my heart sweated tears. My feelings of hatred for them had been the luxury of a hurt child. Actually I loved them much more than I could have thought, and even for Ester I suffered the pain of knowing that her hope might very well have been in vain.

Of course, I had to tell them what I had found out. A realistic appraisal of our situation had to be made. But how? How was I to tell them? I said, "Dad, maybe we should stop listening to the *Judenrat*. They say stay home and pray. But maybe we should fight back and escape." He gave me a scathing look. "The Lord has brought us this far and now will you turn your back on Him? You think the rabbis and our other leaders are fools? Go to bed and I don't want to hear such dangerous talk again." So I went to bed feeling sorrowful, hurt, denied; bottled up with so many feelings I thought I would explode. The following day was the infamous Friday of the German's "final solution" of Bobowa ghetto. All the Jews that remained in the ghetto were loaded up into trucks and taken away. The *Judenrat* ran around trying to calm people, saying: "It's only another ghetto we're moving to. A better one with lots of room and more food. It's all right. Everything is all right. We are only being resettled in the East." The members of the *Judenrat* were Jews just like everyone else and they, too, got into the German military trucks. My stepmother Ester had given me a parting gift, a jewel of sentiment no Nazi could have extracted from her. "Shmulek, I love you" — the words echoed in my head. For all I knew, I was the only Jew in the Bobowa ghetto who did not get onto those military trucks. Desperately, I hoped I had company. Some dear face I longed to see: a relative, a friend, anyone at all.

> How long does it take a sob
> from the belly to reach the throat?
> When is memory put to rest?
> A tear is a diamond,
> each drop a piece of soul:
> and this is the wealth
> of the Jewish people.

* * * * *

I survived the final solution. But at what cost? When would I ever see my family again? The whole of Poland stretched before me filled with a number of unfriendly gentile Poles and Nazis. Where to go — I didn't know; the road to anywhere at all was precarious indeed.

JUZEK* THE PEN KNIFE STEALER

If a crow flew from Bielanka to Gorlice it would pass over the villages of Biesnik and Mszanka along the way. A village was often just a collection of farms and houses at a secluded spot in the countryside, and several villages might be very close together. The villages had thatched roofs, outhouses, and no electricity, running water or paved roads. Bystra was a village near Mszanka and this was where the good peasant woman Balwina lived with her family.

One evening there was a knock at her door. The year was 1942. Poland was in the vise of Nazi occupation. The land was cloaked with fear and one was cautious to answer a knock on one's door. Behind the hand that knocked could be a Gestapo man, a beggar insane with hunger, or worse yet — a Jew. A person got money for turning in a Jew to the Gestapo — in fact, some murderous peasants made a business out of bounty hunting Jewish fugitives. One of these murderers was a peasant called Krupa. If one wasn't careful they could also get marked with suspicion, and it was better to avoid the fugitives altogether. Just a few days before this particular evening the Bobowa ghetto had been evacuated. The Germans had called this operation the "final solution" of the Bobowa ghetto. Many Polish peasants applauded the operation. Some, however, at the risk of their own lives, were righteous, altruistic heroes. They helped the unfortunate victims.

The knock once more sounded at Balwina's door and her husband raised up his voice:

"Who's there?"

"Shmulek. It is Shmulek Oliner."

"Who?"

"Shmulek. Aron's son."

Balwina opened the door. Caught between the lighted kitchen and the darkness of the night she hovered uncertainly. Then she saw it was indeed Shmulek.

"For Heaven's sake, what are you doing here? It's very dangerous. Where did you come from? Hurry, come on in."

The kitchen of this peasant farmhouse had whitewashed walls. There was a shrine in the corner. A cross made of two sticks tied together was on the whitewashed board above the doorway leading to another room. Heat from the oven made the smell of Shmulek's clothing rise dank and foul. Balwina was a big woman with fleshy face and ample bosom. In the manner of a person used to thinking quickly she bolted the door and pulled the shutters over the kitchen window. "What's happened to you?" she said, in mid-stride. "Where're your parents?" Her husband was watching me carefully. He was a thin man with large ears, sitting at the table and smoking a pipe.

"The trucks came to the ghetto and took them away. I don't know where they are or what happened to them. A farmer I met said they were taken to Garbotz. All the Jews were taken to Garbotz and shot!"

"Oh, Shmulek, you dear boy! Whatever has happened to you? You look like you have spent a week hiding in ditches. Come. Did you hear that?" She turned to her husband who was idly puffing on his pipe. "Shmulek ran away from the Bobowa ghetto."

"What did they do to your parents?" he said.

Balwina turned on him. "Oh, you stupid goat. He just said they were shot and now look — you've made him cry! Shmulek, Shmulek . . ." The good peasant

* Juzek is pronounced: Uzak.

woman also cried, reaching out her soft warm arms. "Don't cry, my child. Don't cry. The Lord Jesus will help you. The Lord will help you."

"I had to come here. You were the only person I knew. I had to go somewhere and I was so afraid. I don't believe it. I just don't believe it. They couldn't have killed my parents. I'm sure my parents are somewhere. I have to go look for them. I have . . ."

"No, my child. You stay here. You realize I am endangering my life keeping you here and I'm telling you because I want you out of sight. I want you to stay in the attic. Go up in the attic and stay there until I find out what happened to your parents and what the story is about this thing. Under no circumstances should you show your face outside this house because the neighbors might by spying on me. They know I was the friend of Herman Polster and his son Aron. They might suspect me of being friendly to the Jews and if they saw you here they might turn you in. I don't want Krupa to recognize you because he will deliver you to the Gestapo for sure, and you know what would happen then. That's right, they would shoot us all and maybe even burn down the house."

"Yes, I'll stay up in the attic and hide."

"Now, you must be hungry."

"Yes, I am. All the way from Bobowa I walked and it took me two days. A farmer gave me something to eat and that's all I've had."

The good woman placed some bread and butter and milk on the table. "Here you are child, and don't be afraid to eat all you want."

"Thank you very much."

"Those wretched Germans. Those merciless, brutal Germans. How can they do such a thing to innocent people?" she muttered as she put dishes in a pile to be washed. She brought some more bread to the table. "Here's more food. Don't be afraid to eat. The war may be longer than any of us think and who knows when we'll have full bellies."

"But I heard on the road that the Germans will be defeated in seven weeks. America has entered the war and the Germans will be crushed."

"Don't be so quick to believe it," said Balwina. "The Germans are diabolical geniuses. They spread misinformation among the peasants and no one knows what is happening. I'll bet you didn't know there were ghettos all over Poland? Yes, there were. All over Poland there were ghettos just like Bobowa. Tomorrow I will find out this thing about your parents. Now don't start crying again. There, there. I only want you to be strong and not be quick to believe the war will be easy. If the English and Americans beat the Germans it will be a long hard fight and a lot of good people will die. This is what I think. The only thing for sure in this war is that if you do something the Germans don't like you get shot, so keep your head inside the house. Now finish your bread. That's it — one more piece.

"Good. Now I want you to go up to the attic. There is a bed up there where Staszek, my son, usually sleeps." Balwina looked at me, paused for a second and said to me, "Do you know that my Staszek looks like you?" We will take care of him somewhere else tonight. Now go on up and take off your clothes before getting into bed. You are dirty and smell very bad and I will see to it you have clean clothes in the morning. Good night, now."

The attic was a cold dark place where mice scurried in the corners. The bed was a mattress of straw piled high with blankets and quilts, and underneath this bedding was a little bit of paradise for a body cold and tired to the bone. As comfortable as it was, I couldn't sleep. My mind kept wondering what the future held for me. The next morning bleak grey light came through the cracks between the boards on the wall.

"Shmulek. Hey, Shmulek, come down for breakfast."

The light that came through the cracks in the wall gave little information about the time of day. At the foot of the bed was a pile of clean clothes.

"Good morning."

"Good morning, Shmulek. It's about time you came down out of the attic. Did you sleep well?"

"Yes, thank you. How did those clothes get on the bed?"

Balwina laughed. "You were so sound asleep that a herd of cattle could have walked through the room and you wouldn't have known it." She spoke very lightly but her eyes were red and swollen. "Sit down at the table."

She broke an egg into the frying pan on the stove.

"My husband was out checking around this morning. He talked to the villagers and it's true. The Germans did shoot all the ghetto people. They made them take off their clothes and walk out onto planks and then the machine guns mowed them down. Twenty-one or twenty-two escaped off the military trucks, and the Gestapo are making house-to-house searches for them. It's only about eighteen kilometers from Garbotz to here, Shmulek, and I'm worried for you. You ought to try . . . you know what I suggest to you? You do not look Jewish. You don't have a beard yet and you speak Polish very well, just like a Polish peasant boy. You look just like one of our Polish Christian boys, and I suggest you change your name right now and pretend to be a peasant. Find yourself a job helping out on a farm or tending cows. That's what you should do." She was crying. The egg was burning.

"What happened to my grandparents living in Zyndranowa? Could I go to see them? Could I go stay with Faye and Moishe?"

"Now Shmulek, you are crying just like me. How am I ever going to tell you what happened if you are already crying? I'm sorry the egg is burned. I liked your father, Aron, very much. Herman Polster, you know, helped me out when I was in trouble. He gave me livestock, too. In fact, just before the Germans took his farm away from him he sold me a very fine bullock at a fair price, and gave to me his horse. Those two were very fine men and I feel toward you like a mother. I wish I didn't have such bad news to say."

"What? What is it you are saying?"

"Ah, the Germans are such brutes. There were ghettos all around the country, you know, and each one had its "final solution" by the Germans. Yes, it is a day that the good Lord wept at man's inhumanity to man. One at a time the ghettos were evacuated and the Jews were shot. One after another, and no one knew what was going on, except the Germans. On Thursday a ghetto called Biecz was evacuated and no one passed the word along. No one knew. On Friday the Germans went to Bobowa and no one knew what was happening. I keep saying 'evacuated' and it is because I cannot bring myself to say the word of horrible truth."

"But my grandparents — what happened to Faye and Moishe?"

"Must I tell you? Can't you see by the tears running down my cheeks and guess the truth? There is not a Jew in Poland who is not a fugitive from death itself. You and the Polsters went to the Bobowa ghetto. Faye and Moishe and your family in Zyndranowa went to a ghetto in Dukla. It is all the same. The Germans went from ghetto to ghetto doing what they do so well and now everyone is dead. All your family. Everyone that I know of is dead and the only Jews left alive are fugitives or Jews in concentration camps like Auschwitz, Maidanek, Treblinka, Sobibor, Chelmno and others. That's it, put your head in your arm and cry."

She put the burned egg on a plate and set it on the table.

"In the cities there are bands of Jews fighting underground. There are fugitives hiding in the country. You are too young to fight underground and would probably get killed very quickly. Some peasants everywhere are keeping their eyes out for Jews, because the Gestapo will reward those who capture fugitives with boots and money and things like that. But you do as I tell you and you will live. Only by living will you honor your family and I will help you. If you do what I tell you and change your name and become a Polish boy, no one will know you are a Jew and someday when the war is over you will be grown up and a man and then you can do things to remember your family and tell the world what has happened to your people."

"What type of name . . . who will I . . . what shall I take?"

"How about Jusek . . . Jusek Polewski?"

"O.K. If you think . . . "

"Do you know Polish *paczierz* (prayers)? Daily catechism?

"No, I don't."

"Do you know how to read?"

"No. Polish I cannot read."

"Then I tell you what I will do. I will teach you. You memorize it. And then you go around to the villages near here and look for a job. With what I will teach you, you will seem like a Polish Christian boy. So you just look around for a job and tell everyone who asks that your name is Jusek Polewski.

"And remember — be careful when you undress so that no one will see that you are Jewish. Guard your circumcision because you know what will happen if someone sees it and realizes you are Jewish."

"I will watch myself. I am so grateful to you for doing all this for me — helping me. I don't know what I would have done on my own. I'm scared, though, really scared. Maybe someone will recognize me. I have been in many of the villages around here and it's possible someone will recognize my true identity."

"Don't be afraid. You will act like a Polish gentile boy and if you see anyone you know then avoid that person and watch yourself. Be careful. Now have breakfast."

Realizing that the egg was burned, she made another and put it on the table. Her husband came in from outside. He was much younger than Balwina, uneducated and rather simple. Balwina wore the proverbial pants in the family, and whatever she said was the law. The man walked through the kitchen and into the other room. A boy about eleven years old came into the kitchen followed by a younger girl.

"Staszek," said Balwina, "Sit at the table by Jusek. I might need you to help me. Yes, that's right. Of course, I mean Shmulek."

"Now, Jusek, for that will be your name, let me try to teach you the catechism. O.K., repeat after me: Our Father, who art in Heaven, hallow'd be Thy name. Now remember, repeat after me. Memorize what I say. After you get a job, try to go to church every Sunday."

"Our Father, who art in Heaven, hallow'd be Thy name . . . ."

* * * * *

The days passed, and early one morning Balwina climbed the stairs to the attic. She was still in her nightshirt. The roosters had not yet crowed, and she gently shook the shoulder of Jusek Polewski.

"Wake up, Jusek. Wake up. Remember now, your name is no longer Shmulek Oliner. Jusek, it's dawn outside in just a short while and if you hurry no one will be able to recognize you. I want you to go. Leave this village now. Go to some other village and look for a job. Go from house to house and ask if anyone needs a *pastuch* (cow hand or stable boy)." She began to cry. "I will miss you. Be careful. If you ever . . . if it's safe — but only if it's safe — try to come back some night and visit and tell me where you are. Now be very careful because you know what that means to us."

"Of course. I know what would happen if anyone found out and I will be very careful. I am grateful to you for letting me stay. I am very, very grateful. And someday, if ever I survive this, I will never forget you."

* * * * *

A boy of twelve has lots of imagination. But reality was quick and sharp to cut these fantasies in half. Tears are a funny thing. You imagine things and the horror makes you cry until you think there are no tears left. Then you find out the truth and there are plenty of tears all over again. Balwina told me of the execution at the forest of Garbotz where my family and my people were stripped of their clothing that cold, cold day and told to walk the wooden planks. And for days, it seemed, I cried. A thought or a word — anything at all — sparked the feeling of agony. Balwina was always there, moving about like the mother I didn't have. Two mothers I had had and both were dead. Life seemed unbearably cruel. Balwina said Jewish fugitives were doing whatever they could just to stay alive, and as quickly as I could, I had learned the Christian catechism.

The agony never went away but the tears stopped and rarely after that did I cry again. Just to survive each day took supreme effort and there was no time for tears. The Germans were everywhere and Balwina was afraid I would be found out if I stayed with her. She said: change your name. Learn the catechism. Pretend to be a peasant boy and go to church every Sunday." I felt, partly, that she expected properties my grandfather had owned. Already she had his horse and other presents. Also, she was very religious and quite likely sought the religious reward of converting an infidel. For the most part, however, she was a humanitarian woman with a great, kindly heart. In order to help save another person's life, she was risking her own and her family's lives during the entire period of my acquaintanceship with her.

Walking barefooted on the road leading away from Bystra, the village where Balwina lived, I was certainly not an unusual sight. Since the Germans had entered Poland, a lot of homes had been broken up. Orphaned children were frequently seen on the roads and the Poles generally treated me well. I hitchhiked along the road and the peasants picked me up in their awkward wooden carts. They shared with me their black-crusted bread and joked in a friendly manner.

Disregarding their kindness, I lived in the constant fear of being found out. I imagined how glad these poor friendly Poles would be for a pair of boots or a few hundred *(zlotys)*. Some Poles like Krupa sometimes crippled a captive just for fun before delivering him to the Gestapo, and I vividly imagined this done to myself.

The premature death of my mother had saved her much sorrow and I wondered if she was watching over me. It began to occur to me that death was, indeed, forever. In fact, it seemed death was the only certainty there was. And if death was forever, then there had to be some meaning to the shortness of life — there must be some hope in living. I tried to remember what my mother looked like. But there was just an impression, the smell of *Shabbat* bakings. Even the face of Ester, my stepmother, was sliding away, sliding into the sound of a harsh voice, the look of fear, the touch of last minute tenderness. Also sliding away was Shmulek Oliner. He was a thing of the past buried in the memories of people now dead.

A friendly peasant had given me a ride and in the village of Ropa I hopped off the cart. Away he went, sitting up there on the wagon seat behind the plodding horse. From house to house I went, asking if anyone had need of a *pastuch*, a cowhand. No luck. I picked apples that still clung to the trees at this late season and ate them for my lunch. From the fields I pulled carrots. Night descended quickly and I crawled into a peasant's barn and hid in the hay. Sometimes a snoopy dog would discover my presence in the barn and bark without letting up. When that happened I had to move on and find a more friendly barn.

Sometimes in those barns, in the middle of the night, I woke up covered with sweat. I had dreamed that the Gestapo was chasing me and had finally trapped me in Balwina's house. My father was there and I turned to him for help. He told me to leave him alone and I screamed: "I hate you!" Then my heart broke because even more than I hated him — I loved him. This I tried to tell him but my efforts were futile. No amount of entreaty seemed to have an effect on him. Then I realized he was dead.

The rich warm smell of animal manure reminded me I was not at Balwina's house but sleeping in a peasant's barn in the village of Ropa. For a moment I let myself think my life might be a dream within a dream, and that I might wake up in England or America or some other safe place. But such thoughts were luxuries hardly to be afforded, and I stopped thinking them right away.

The next morning I got up before dawn. The farmhouse windows were yellow with light. Across some low hills I made my way and finally ended up in a village called Biesnik. By now the sun had risen and at the first farm I came to the farmer was just letting his cows out of their stables and driving them to the nearby pastures.

"Do you know who needs a *pastuch*?"

He leaned on the wooden side of a stable and squinted at me. Cold air was coming through the open barn door, and the manure in the stable was steaming.

"Yes, I know of such a place. You go up about ten houses. There is a large house there that used to belong to a Jew. A man named Padworski lives there now; he and his wife. You'll find he's a nice man and I just happen to know he needs a *pastuch*. You tell him that I, Woitek, sent you and he will talk to you."

"Thank you very much."

"Good luck."

At a brisk pace I set off down the dirt road counting the houses as I went. Each number I had to repeat several times in my mind because the houses were far apart and I didn't want to lose count. Wild bleak grass grew along the side of the dirt road. There were no wires for electricity as there had been in Dukla. The houses didn't have modern plumbing. There were no German motorcars roaring down the dirt road; and the morning rested peacefully in the stillness of the earth. For a moment, I stopped and stood as still as a piece of grass that glistened in the rising sun. These quiet moments I began to collect and appreciate for I didn't know how many of them I would ever have.

The tenth house from where Woitek lived turned out to be a snug farm. There was the house, a barn, and a small cherry and apple orchard. Under a large shade tree next to the house was the entrance to a cellar dug into the ground. Even if Woitek hadn't told me the Padworski's lived on a Jewish farm, I would have known. The wooden fence surrounding the lawn reminded me of my grandparents' farm in Zyndranowa. A small dog ran limping on one foot out of the barn and barked at my approach.

The house door was open and I took my cap off and stuck my head inside. A man was sitting at the table in the kitchen. Through the window next to the table sunlight shone on the newspaper he was reading. The air outside was cool but warming with the sun.

"Mr. Padworski? Are you Mr. Padworski? Woitek from down the road sent me to you because he, I mean, he told me you might be needing a *pastuch*. I have experience with animals and I can tell you I will work very hard."

The man put down the newspaper and turned toward me. The hair and sideburn on one side of his head were illuminated by the sun and his eyes were blue and looked very cool. Shrinking back a little I thought: 'I can't go through with this. The Jew who used to own this farm is dead and if this gentile Pole finds out I am Jewish, I, too, will end up dead.'

"Yes, son. As a matter of fact we are looking for a *pastuch*. How old are you?"

"Thirteen, sir."

"Thirteen? My, you don't look thirteen. What's your name?"

"My name is Jusek Polewski."

"Hmmmm. Never heard of you, Jusek. Where do you live?"

"I'm from Lyrżna."

"Lyrżna. That's very strange. Where is that? What are you doing so far away from home?"

"Oh, I . . . I came looking for work from village to village."

"Where are your parents?"

"My father is dead. My mother lives in Lyrżna with my brother. She is very poor and there is not enough food for everyone in the house and she told me to look for work. So I was going village to village. I've just been to Ropa and there was nothing there for me to do so I thought I would try here."

The door opened and a woman walked into the kitchen. She looked rather young, with a broad face and blonde hair tied with a handkerchief.

"You know, honey, this boy wants to be our *pastuch*. I think we need one, don't you agree?"

The woman looked at me and smiled.

"Hello, son."

"Hello, Mrs. Padworski."

She turned to the man sitting at the table.

"Oh, yes, definitely. We could use a *pastuch*. He looks like a strong boy."

"Thank you. I will work very hard. I can harness horses and drive carts and plow fields and milk cows. I can clean horses and take them to the fields for grazing. There are alot of things I know how to do. And I can keep the stable clean."

"Yes, but you're so young and I don't know how much you would be wanting for work like that," said Mr. Padworski.

"Oh, I don't want much."

"Tell you what," said Mr. Padworski. "You can start working now, but in a few weeks I want you to go back to Lyrżna and bring to me your mother so that we can negotiate."

"Sure, I'll do that. If you want to talk to her, I'll bring her to you and then you can do these negotiations."

Mrs. Padworski squeezed her hands together and smiled at me.

"I'm so glad!" she said. "I think you will like it here with us. We have no children of our own. And as long as you do your work well and obey and respect my husband, then I'm sure we will all get on very well."

"Thank you very much, Mrs. Padworski." I took her hand and kissed it gratefully. She smiled a little nervously and said, "Well, let me . . . let me show you where you are going to sleep. We don't have any room in the house. Let me take you to the stable. There is a bed in the corner of the stable and you can sleep there. I don't have any blankets but there's lots of hay and soft straw."

"Thank you very much. That will be just fine. Many times I have slept on straw and it is a very good thing."

She showed me the stable and then I had the rest of the day to wander about the farm getting used to it. That night as I lay in the stable I thought of the Padworskis and what I had learned about them. They were of aristocratic background. While they were not Nazi sympathizers, they certainly showed no love for the Jews. In fact, Mr. Padworski was an engineer and had had some litigations with Jewish businesses. The farm had belonged to a Mr. Herman Shiff who was also driven out to the Bobowa ghetto at the same time as my family, and who also died at Garbotz. The Padworskis rented it from the occupying German government in power. Mr. Padworski was not actually a farmer by trade but was a city dweller. In addition to his engineering work he had paper work of some kind to do, and as his *pastuch*, much of the farm work would rest on my shoulders. The stable was odorous and very warm with animal heat. Lying on a bed made of a few wooden planks covered with straw, I prayed that no one would find out that I was Jewish.

The next morning I woke up early. Mrs. Padworski came out to the barn and milked the cows. She sang a little as she squirted milk in the bucket and flashed a smile at me when I said good morning. Then she set the bucket aside and winked at me as she walked to the back of the barn. She squatted out of sight in a particular stall and I wondered what she could possibly be doing, because the stall was empty. Presently, she came out of the stall. Gently she put her hand on my shoulder and led me out to the field where the cows were grazing. After pointing out where the cows were not allowed to go, she walked back to the farm. There was no fence separating the pasture from the field of grain and I spent the morning making sure the cows stayed in the grass.

At noontime I drove the cows as far away from the grain as possible and returned to the farm for lunch. As I neared the house I saw a shiny black Gestapo car leaving the driveway. My heart seemed to trip a beat and sweat stood out on my forehead. With weak knees I entered the house; my mouth felt like it was filled with dust. Mr. and Mrs. Padworski were sitting at the table staring down at the table top. They seemed very tense and neither one looked up at me. Mr. Padworski turned his cold blue eyes on me and my stomach seemed to pour down into my legs. I stammered:

"The cows, the cows they are — "

"Jusek, I have something to ask you."

"Uhhh . . . "

"Jusek, do you have a knife?"

"N-no, sir."

Mrs. Padworski spoke up: "Well, have you got a penknife on you?"

"No, ma'm. I don't have a penknife on me. I don't own a knife."

"Did you own a knife before?"

"Yes. Once I had one. But not now. I must have lost the one I had a long time ago."

"We just wondered. We thought you might have a knife with you."

Silently I bowed my head and ate bread and butter with a bowl of soup. Mrs. Padworski continued:

"How do you like our cows? Aren't they nice fat Jewish cows?"

"What do you mean they're Jewish?"

"Oh, they were left here when Herman Shiff was sent to the ghetto and we got the farm. We are renting this farm from the government."

"Oh, is that right? I didn't know," I lied. "I thought you owned the farm."

"Not at all. This was a Jewish farm."

Mr. Padworski said, "The Jews have caused me much trouble in the past but now I feel sorry for what has happened to them."

"The house is very nice," I said.

"Yes," said Mrs. Padworski. "It is the nicest house here. It is well kept, not like some of the other houses in the village. Did you know that some of the other houses in the village are like stables? Some of the farmers keep cows and horses right in the same room where they sleep."

"I know that, yes, because in my village some farmers do the same thing. I've seen goats, for instance, and sheep in the same room as people."

"What village did you say you were from?"

"I'm from Lyrżna."

"Lyrżna. Oh yes, now I remember, I've heard of it. It's not far from Bobowa, isn't that right?"

"Yes, that's right."

"Don't you miss your mother?"

"I guess I do miss her. But I'll get used to it. I like it here. This is a very nice house and you are very good to me. I've never seen a nice house like this before."

As quickly as possible I finished eating and took up my cap. Outside I breathed more easily but I was so scared that I could hardly think straight. Briefly, I considered running away. But then came the realization that if the Padworskis knew I was a Jew I was done for. They would spread the word and every Pole in the country would be looking for a Jewish boy who looked just like me. Then I would not find work as a *pastuch*. Most likely a Gestapo bullet would finish me off. And I decided the best thing I could do would be to hold on to the identity already established and try to convince the Padworskis of it.

In the evening I took the cows back to the stable. Mrs. Padworski milked them and not once did she smile at me. When I went into the house Mr. Padworski greeted me very coldly. Were the Gestapo in the next room, I would not have been surprised. After dinner I excused myself and went out to the barn.

The next morning I got the same cold feelings from the Padworskis. If they suspected I was Jewish, I couldn't figure out what they were waiting for. A word to the Gestapo was all that was needed to end the affair. I wondered, 'Is it possible they are very cruel people after all and keeping me on edge?' Mrs. Padworski acted as if I had done her a personal injury. At breakfast I was so nervous I could hardly eat. Mr. Padworski lifted his eyes from the newspaper he was reading and gave me an "I know all about you" look; and when I pushed open the kitchen door in order to drive the cows out to the field, the perspiration on the palm of my hand left a print on the door.

For a long time I considered not going back to the farm at noon. But I had already decided not to run away. And if I didn't return to the farm for lunch the suspicions concerning me might very well be increased. So I did, in fact, go back, but I was in such a scared condition I didn't see how I could possibly keep any food in my stomach.

Mrs. Padworski was waiting for me in the stable.

"You know something, Jusek? I have a very unusual story to tell you."

An instant sweat came over me. Right then and there I wanted to beg her not to turn me over to the Gestapo, but my tongue was stuck to the roof of my mouth and wouldn't make a sound. She said:

"Do you remember yesterday we kept asking you about a penknife and you said you didn't have one? Well, my husband had a very beautiful penknife which had sentimental value and it was stolen by Jusek."

"Which Jusek?"

"Jusek Szlachta."

"Oh, is that right? I didn't know that."

"He was here yesterday morning. He came to ask for something and he was inside the house and saw it on the mantelpiece and took it — this beautiful knife — and do you know that last night I had a dream that it was he who took the knife, and I went over to his house this morning and said: 'Jusek, can I have my husband's penknife back?' And his mother took it out of his pocket and gave it to me. Jusek Polewski, we thought it was you who took the knife and you know what we were planning to do with you?"

"No. What would you have done?"

"We were planning to fire you, to tell you to go, because we thought you were a thief."

"Oh, I'm so sorry you had to think that. I never stole anything in my life!"

"I know, dear, and I'm ashamed we suspected you. I'm sorry we thought you might be a thief. Can you ever forgive us? I know you are a hard working *pastuch*."

"Thank you. I'll try and work hard for you. I know you won't be sorry for hiring me."

She left the stable and went into the house. So great was my relief I started trembling. For several minutes I just sat on the straw in the stable and trembled. Finally, I got a hold of myself and walked into the house for lunch. Mr. Padworski smiled broadly at me and patted my back.

"You're all right, son. Just keep up the good work."

One thing still bothered me very much.

"Was that the Gestapo I saw here yesterday at noon?"

Mr. Padworski laughed. For the past day everything had been tense; now he was trying to make up with me, and in a sense, everything was funny.

"Oh, yes. That was just the Gestapo looking for some Jews. Some Jews escaped from the ghetto, you know, and the Gestapo was hunting them down."

I swallowed a mouthful of soup and felt it travel all the way down my throat. From the corner of my eye I looked at him. "Maybe they should hire dogs for that," he continued, "To hunt for Jews like they hunt for rabbits and foxes." He was goading me, trying to make me laugh. Only the coldness of his eyes disconcerted me. And I could never be quite certain he did not, in fact, suspect I was Jewish.

Mrs. Padworski said, "Do you know that the Germans are advancing into Russia? They claim they're going to defeat Russia completely in another three to four weeks."

I thought: 'God, what will that mean to me? What will that mean to Jews all over the world if the Germans win the war?'

Mr. Padworski leaned back in his chair and smoked a homemade cigarette. I finished my lunch and returned to the fields.

THE DEAD ARE WATCHING US

One Friday afternoon I was tending the cows on the rugged mountain pasture above the Padworski farm. The pasture land was divided into patches of grass and grain and potatoes; and as I watched the cows to make sure they stayed in the grass, I thought how clever animals can be. Each cow seemed to have a mind of its own, and edged closer and closer to the grain to get a mouthful on the sly. Sometimes the cows would go in different directions, so that while one was stealing mouthfuls from one forbidden patch, diverting my attention, another could steal something from another forbidden patch.

With me was Jusek Szlachta, who had stolen Mr. Padworski's penknife. He often played with me while I watched the cows and, although I didn't trust him, I liked his company. He always seemed curious about my origins and I had to be careful not to contradict myself (a thousand times, at least, I had to repeat I was from Lyrżna). I often worried that if someone lived in Biesnik who came from Lyrżna, they could tell the Padworskis that there is no Polewski family living in Lyrżna. Also, I had to be careful about my circumcision. This was sometimes difficult to do, as he was fond of taking off his clothes and exposing himself to the sun. Our conversations usually centered around girls and sex.

He offered me a cigarette, made by himself out of clover and pieces of newspaper, and I accepted it.

"Have you heard of the Jews who escaped from the jail? The Gestapo are looking for them."

"Oh yeah," I said. "That happened a long time ago. Mr. Padworski told me all about it."

"Well, I hope they find them and clean them all up. Then we'll have a Jew-free Poland." He watched my face for a reaction. "My father said that before the war all the wealth was in Jewish hands. The priest . . . Hey, you're not paying attention! Yeah, the priest said the Jews killed Jesus Christ. Did you know that?"

"Of course," I said. "Everyone knows that."

And I wondered how long I would live if he knew I was a Jew? I anticipated each step he would take to finish me off. First, he would go to his dirty house with a cow in the bedroom along with everyone else and announce the discovery to his father. Then he would go to the Gestapo station in Gorlice, report me and get the reward. The Gestapo man would come to Biesnik in his big black car, catch me and tell me to take off my pants. When he had seen the circumcision, I would be taken to Gestapo headquarters, tortured and asked where other Jews were hiding. After the Gestapo was through with me, I would be taken to a Jewish cemetery and told to dig my own grave, as were a number of other Jews I had heard about. Then I would be told to lie down, facing the bottom, and they would shoot me . . . I shook my head in order to recover from this dismal imagination. Fortunately, I was on the hillside and not in the Jewish cemetery.

My eyes traversed to the right as I watched the cows grazing. Each movement brought them closer to a large patch of grain. And I thought: 'It would not be a bad life, being a cow.'

"What are you thinking about?" said Jusek.

"Oh, nothing in particular. I was thinking wouldn't it be nice if the Germans were driven out of Poland and Poland were free again."

"My father says pretty soon the Germans will be defeated by the English and the Americans."

"I certainly hope so because the Germans are really occupying our land."

"Do you hate the Germans?"

"Sure, I hate the Germans," I said. "They're occupying our land."

"Yeah, I hate the Germans, too. But they've done a good thing for us. They've cleaned out the Jews."

"Yeah, I guess that's the best thing they could have done for us."

"Did you know they killed a lot of Jews at Garbotz?"

"Sure. Who doesn't know that?"

"They were shooting all day long. I have a cousin who heard the machine guns going for a very long time. Imagine killing that many people in one grave?! You know, it took the farmers in that area two months just to dig the hole for all those Jews?"

"Those Germans took care of everything. They have such fine, fast machine guns." I looked around to change the subject. It was a little warmer. Clouds appeared in the distance along the horizon and Jusek commented on them:

"I bet it's going to storm tonight." Then he said, "Are you going to church this Sunday?"

"To church? Oh yes, sure. I go to church every now and then."

"I go to church every Sunday," he said, giving me a sly look. "I'm a real good Catholic. Are you a Catholic, too?"

"Of course I'm a Catholic."

I looked around to change the subject again and saw a man walking toward me. As he got nearer I started shaking from fright because the face was familiar. It was the face of a Jew. He had lived right next to us in the Bobowa ghetto and knew me very well. In fact, he was our landlord. Upon seeing me, he stood still for a moment.

"Shmul . . . Shm . . ."

Waving my hand at him, I quickly turned my back and said to Jusek, "Jusek, please do me a favor, will you boy, and get that cow out of the oats? See, she's eating up the oats!"

Jusek did as I asked him and ran to get the cow. I walked over to the Jew I had recognized and said, "Simcha, please, please leave me alone. Nobody knows I am Jewish here. You are going to give me away. I'll tell you what; you run into the woods and hide there. At night I'll bring you some food."

"O.K. I'll see you tonight behind that hill."

Jusek drove the cow out of the oats. Then he came running back looking after the man who was walking away.

"Who was that man?"

"I don't know. He said he was lost and looking for directions."

"Was he Jewish? He looked like he could have been Jewish."

"I don't know. Why don't you run after him and ask?"

"This is no joking matter. A Jew is worth a lot of money."

"Sometimes you are really stupid, Jusek. Why would a Jew walk around in broad daylight?"

"Oh — yeah." He scuffed the ground with his foot. "I guess you're right. No Jew would be that dumb."

We sat down on the grass and watched the cows. Nonchalantly they grazed tearing loose the grass with their strong, square teeth. They didn't care that I was a

Jew. Neither did they care that Jusek was a Jew-hater; and had I died right before their eyes, they probably would not have stopped grazing. How maddening it sometimes was being human! Jusek and I were each caught in our private thoughts and I worried about what his might be. After what seemed an eternity of silence, he brought up the topic of girls.

That night I sneaked away from the farm and went to the woods. I met Simcha behind the little hill he had pointed out earlier. Eagerly he ate the potatoes and bread I had brought. I knew he was starving. So few of my people did I see, I felt for him as I would toward a brother and steadied his shoulder with my hand.

"How did you run away? How did you escape from the Germans?"

"I climbed through the fence before the shooting," he said.

"Do you know what happened to my parents?"

"No, Shmulek, I don't. All I know is that the Jews were loaded into trucks and transported all day to Garbotz and shot there. I think your parents were, too."

"What will happen, Simcha . . . what will happen to us?"

"I don't know. Maybe the Germans will be defeated soon. In the meantime, just try to hold out. In the meantime . . . I don't know." He had eaten everything I had brought. The night was very dark but I could see his face clearly. He was staring at the moon and the whites of his eyes glistened.

"Listen," he said. "I will tell you a story. I met another Jew on the road. His beard was tangled and filled with spittle. His eyes were wide with a constant state of horror and he cried out with fear at his own imaginations. At first I thought he was one of those afflicted from birth, that the war has turned loose from their families. Then, between outbursts, he told me his story."

"From what he said and what I could piece together, he was one of those taken to Garbotz. It was a big hole waiting there for all those Jews. The busy hands that dug it must have worked a long, long time. The German butchers couldn't shoot the Jews and bury them fast enough. Our people lay in that hole dead and wounded and some just fainted from shock. The Germans couldn't bury them fast enough, so over these people. many of them not even dead, the butchers poured a chemical."

Like the eyes of a wild animal, Simcha's eyes reflected the moon.

"But this particular Jew who was now a madman happened to be near the top. The German guards had more important things to do than hang around and listen to the moans of dying people, so this Jew escaped by climbing out of the hole and running into the woods. In that hole filled with blood, excrement and bodies, he left his sanity. I tried to do something for him but he was beyond help. It was only a matter of time before somebody turned him in for a pair of boots from the Gestapo; I thought the best thing I could do for him was to catch a few of the butchers and do to them as they had done to countless Jews who had never done anything to hurt them. As soon as it is dawn I will leave this area for Gorlice where I hope to find the Jewish underground."

He turned his glowing eyes upon me.

"I tell you this for a reason. You are lucky. You have a good cover here on this Polish farm. And you must remember: if you survive the war you must not forget your people. You must tell tales of horror. We must avenge the innocent. Our leaders and rabbis gave us bad advice about the Germans. They should have told us to arm ourselves and fight the Nazis. But the rabbis were holy men and they have died with their people. The leaders of the *Judenrat* did what they could for us in their own way, and they, too, have paid the price of being Jewish."

"You must remember what the Germans have done to us. We must never forget because the dead are watching us. The world must be told about Nazi bestiality. But first of all you must live. You are very young ... and perhaps that is to your advantage. Good luck."

"Simcha, you must know I have a different name. I'm called Jusek Polewski. If you ever have to come to me for food, do come. But make sure no one else is around. Talk to me secretly and I'll bring you food at night. Good luck."

"Good luck to you, Jusek Polewski."

As I walked back toward the farm I noticed the lantern in the barn was lit. The last hundred yards I sprinted. Inside the barn, Mr. Padworski was in the stall with one of the cows. Mrs. Padworski was holding the lantern, and they both looked at me accusingly.

"Where have you been?" shouted Mr. Padworski. Rarely did he raise his voice and I was scared to death.

"Here it is the middle of the night and you are out running around. Is there something going on I should know about? Or maybe you can explain why the cow is calving and you are not here to help?"

Without waiting for a reply from me, he turned his attention to the cow. Numbly, I helped. A short time later, he smiled proudly at the slimy wet calf that lay on the straw.

"I'm sorry, Jusek," he said, ruffling my hair. "I didn't mean to get so angry a little while ago. It was just that the cow was having trouble and I was concerned and needed help and you were nowhere to be found." He laughed with relief, then mused quietly, "I don't think I'll report this calf to the Germans. Why feed a good calf to some German belly?"

"By the way, Jusek, where were you tonight?"

Immediately, I broke out with perspiration. An explanation stuck in my throat, and not knowing what else to do, I walked to the calf and stroked its head which was still wet and very silky. Mrs. Padworski brought the lantern close to the calf and crooned softly laying her hand on my shoulder. My heart was pounding and I wrestled desperately with a possible explanation should Mr. Padworski ask his question again. But his mind seemed to be on other things; he said something to Mrs. Padworski and they left the barn and walked to the house.

Not until the kitchen door closed did I sigh with relief. And this sigh was a very short one. The following day would hold new dangers for me, I was sure, and I readied myself with an explanation for my absence from the barn.

Fortunately. Mr. Padworski seemed to forget all about the incident and the farm work continued as usual. I had to clean the stables, feed the cattle, and help with the harvesting. When the new calf learned to walk, it followed me around everywhere I went and before long we were good friends.

The Poles were not allowed to slaughter cattle. Rabbits, however, were an allowable source of meat and one of my duties on the farm was to kill rabbits for the Padworskis. To do this, I would pick the animal up by a hind leg and hit it with a stick right behind the ears. Then I would drop it behind me and assume it was dead.

One time, I had to kill four rabbits for a special meal and turned around to find one missing. Apparently, I hadn't hit it hard enough, and it wobbled to a bunch of hay and hid. The situation was very moving. The creature seemed almost human. I felt he was hurt enough that he would probably die of pain. Searching through the hay I finally found him screaming as if to beg for mercy. So I left him alone and strangely enough he recovered and lived a long time.

Feeling elated that I had helped preserve a life of some kind, I went to find my friend the calf. Between us was a tenderness and I talked to the calf and told it secrets quite as if it could understand. Nowhere was my friend to be found. I searched in the barn for the second time. Then outside the barn and out in back of the house. Usually when I called the calf's name it came running. Now there returned to me only the plaintiveness of my voice.

With a heavy heart I went to the farmhouse for my evening meal. Not only had I lost a friend but the calf had belonged to Mr. Padworski; how would I explain to him the loss of such valuable livestock? Mr. Padworski and I sat at the table waiting for Mrs. Padworski to bring the food. As usual, he was reading his newspaper, the *Krakauer Zeitung* (Cracow News), a German language propaganda newspaper. Over the top of the newspaper he peered at me.

"Jusek, did you know the Gestapo is looking for a Jew reported to be in this area? On the road to Gorlice they captured a Jew from the Bobowa ghetto. They did some terrible things to him, and before they ended his misery, he reported having had contact with another Jewish fugitive. Do you think he would have held up under Gestapo torture?"

"I d-don't know."

"Not at all. The Germans are very good at extracting any information they might want." His wife set a platter of steaming meat on the table. She cast a look at me and walked quickly away. He continued, "And in our very midst — our geographic area, that is — we have a fugitive. I am not interested in any Gestapo reward. On the other hand, it would not be good for a Jew to be discovered on our property, and I want you to keep your eyes open." Very quickly I realized he wasn't talking about me. I was staring at the platter of meat on the table. "This Jew is reportedly a madman and, — Jusek . . . Jusek?"

He noticed my focus of attention. He put his paper down and cleared his throat. His wife came to the table and sat with her head quietly bowed. My forehead burned hot and a wall of water seemed to rise within me choking me and making my ears roar. I felt I would burst for sure but my eyes remained dry.

"Jusek, I thought perhaps you would take this well. We're in a war you know. People are dying everywhere. The Germans make us register our cattle and take our surplus beef. We who are alive must eat to stay alive and for a long time we've had nothing but a bland diet."

My eyes filled with water and I fought to keep the water from spilling over.

"The calf wasn't registered you know."

"Jusek, eat," said Mrs. Padworski. "It's for your health."

The blood that had burned up into my forehead seemed to leave my body altogether and I felt faint. Numbly, I excused myself and left the table. As the cool evening air hit my face, I got myself under control. But my ears still roared loudly and I was in a state of confusion. Behind a bush, I vomited. I could not eat the calf who had been my friend. As I walked to the barn, I bitterly murmered the name, "Simcha." For a moment, I thought I would tell everyone I was a Jew just to shake them up. Of course, such a move would be fatal. And as my strength waned, the words Simcha had spoken to me arose to give me comfort.

As if the thought of the slaughtered calf was not enough, the Padworskis received an order from the German army to deliver one of its two cows to Bobowa for slaughter. The German army had all the cattle in Poland registered so that they knew at a glance what meat inventory they had on hand. Mr. Padworski had no choice but to choose one cow and deliver it to Bobowa as ordered. Suddenly it occurred to me that he would want me to go on the two day walking trip to Bobowa. Sweat came over me as I thought: 'What if someone recognizes me there, or what if Mr. Padworski wants to accompany me along the journey?' Quickly, another horrible thought unfolded before me: Lyrżna, the village that I purportedly came from lay on the very road to Bobowa. What if Mr. Padworski wanted to stop in my village and meet my mother and talk with her about me? As I feared, Mr. Padworski announced that we would take the old cow (which I considered the smarter one) and we would both go to Bobowa to deliver it and get the proper receipts from the German authorities. He added, "That way we will be passing through your village Lyrżna and can see your mother."

I looked at him pretending that I was pleased with his suggestions.

Early Thursday morning we took sandwiches, put a rope on the cow's neck and began to walk in the direction of Bobowa. The cow refused to move. I pulled her by the rope and Mr. Padworski beat her with a stick. Reluctantly, she moved slowly up a ridge in the direction of Bobowa. I felt she had a cow's premonition that this was the end for her, too. My confused mind kept racing about what to do with my own predicament. What excuses would I offer to Mr. Padworski this time about my lies if he should discover them?

The cow didn't want to move quickly. The walk towards Bobowa kept slowing down and with a sudden jerk the cow got loose and began to gallop back towards Biesnik. I gave chase. Mr. Padworski couldn't because he had angina pectoris. I caught the cow and we marched on.

Night kept creeping up on us and it was decided that we would spend the night by a creek, still about 10 kilometers away from Lyrżna and about 20 kilometers from Bobowa. The cow grazed, Mr. Padworski slept, and I kept thinking of a way out of my immanent discovery.

The next morning, we woke, ate our stale sandwiches and marched on. We had to hurry because the orders stated that we had to have the cow in Bobowa by nightfall on Friday. We arrived at Lyrżna. Mr. Padworski asked: "Where is your mother's house?" I pointed in some direction six kilometers away from where we were and said, "My house is in that forest."

He quickly said, "That's quite far. We can't stop now because of time pressure."

A load was lifted off my anxious body.

We arrived at Bobowa and fortunately it was beginning to get dark and cloudy. 'Good,' I thought to myself, 'The darkness will hide me and we will get out of Bobowa under the cover of night." We delivered the reluctant and tired old Jewish cow. She mooed and kicked and looked in our direction. I felt badly inside my heart. Mr. Padworski said, "Goodbye, you poor old *Zosia*," (that was her nickname), "You have served us well." He, too, was capable of grief, I noticed.

"Off we go back to Lyrżna," he said. My anxiety renewed itself as I glanced at Bobowa, memories of misery raced before my eyes. It was only two years ago that I escaped from this hell hole. Now it appeared life had returned there. Only now it had no Jews but gentiles that took over the Jewish houses. The ghetto was no more, and fences that enclosed the Jews were also largely dismantled. Mr. Padworski was

74

tired and coughed **a lot** as we walked back in the direction of Lyrżna. He suggested that we rest and spend the night under the nearby orchard trees.

Next morning early, we got up and noticed heavy clouds covering the sky. Mr. Padworski said, "You know, Jurek, let's move on and save time. You won't mind if we don't stop at your mother's place?"

I was overjoyed with his statement, though I tried not to show it. I added, "That seems like a good idea. We would have to go about 10 kilometers out of our way, and my mother is probably at work in the field at one of the rich peasant's farm." 'My God,' I thought to myself, 'What a narrow escape!' We arrived tired and sad at Biesnik thinking of poor *Zosias'* fate.

THEY FOUGHT BACK

"Jusek, you know it's time for you to go get your mother so we can negotiate. Then we'll know exactly what we'll have to pay you for working here."

"Oh, there's no hurry. My mother will . . . there's no rush — uh — I think maybe we ought to wait 'til — oh, when I make a trip home around Christmas time. Don't you think that would be a good idea? We have much work to do here on the farm and really I should stay here. Until Christmas I could work for room and board."

"Don't you miss your mother, boy?" said Mrs. Padworski, looking at me with a mixture of pity and fondness. I liked her very much. She seemed to have accepted me as a son, of inferior caliber to be sure. She seemed to have other feelings for me as well, which sometimes made me nervous. For instance, instead of using the outhouse, which was very cold, she would often come out to the barn. After a while I learned not to pay attention. But I was disturbed nonetheless.

"Sure I miss my mother," I said, avoiding her probing eyes. "But my family is very poor. They rely on me. And now I have responsibilities here, too. Somehow, my mother will get the money she needs and I will get my work done, too. Without me to feed, she will be all right. And when we get the negotiations straightened out she will get all that money and it will be a happy day."

"All right," said Mr. Padworski. "If that's the way you want it. You can work for your room and board for the time being. And when I meet your mother we'll decide."

There was a long silence while he read the newspaper. I was sitting in the corner by the stove. His wife was also reading the paper.

"Yah," said Mr. Padworski, "It looks like the Germans are having some trouble in Stalingrad. That's what it says here, anyway, and you know very well that if the Germans admit to having some trouble they must be having it indeed."

"I hope so," said his wife. "I hope they're having good trouble, good and plenty. You know, there's an article here how some Jews escaped from the Gestapo. Imagine, from the Gestapo itself!"

"Fantastic! How could the Jews have done that — to escape from the Germans?"

Well, it says here they were betrayed by a . . . some girl. I'm not sure who this girl was; maybe the lover of one of the men? You know the Germans are very good, it seems, at getting someone to talk. Anyway, they were taken to the Gestapo headquarters where they were undressed and they were just about to be taken to the cemetery when they escaped in their underwear. Tell me, do they — the Germans I mean — take Jews who are still alive to the cemetery?"

"Never mind," said Mr. Padworski. "Not now. What else happened?"

"One of the Jews hit a guard — a German guard."

"Good for the Jew. At least when they hang up his hide he'll have that against the Germans. Do we know him? Do we know any of those Jews?"

"Apparently they are local. The sons of a man named Shiff." She looked at her husband a bit quizzically. "I wonder if they could be . . . Tell me, did the Shiff who owned this farm have any sons?"

Her husband seemed preoccupied and didn't answer the question. Perhaps the question had occurred to him and he was trying to answer it for himself. One thing

76

these Poles who lived in Jewish farms and houses had not yet had to face was the problem of the rightful Jewish owners on the loose.

She finally broke the silence with a reminiscent tone: "I wonder what the rest of the world will say to Germany, how the rest of the world will express feelings toward Germany, about the fact that they've destroyed the Jews and gypsies so mercilessly and butchered so many millions of other innocent people?"

"Oh, I don't know. If the Germans ever lose the war I think the American Jews will really try to make them repay all the damages. Yeah, the American Jews and those in England, too, will not like the Germans very much. Did you know there are five million Jews in America? And most of them are wealthy!"

From the corner where I was sitting I spoke up. "Is that really true? I didn't know that." My hands were still held out to the hot iron of the stove and my clothing facing the stove was toasty.

He turned including me in the conversation for the first time. "Well, I'm sure there's a lot you don't know," he said with a frown, as if he thought my tone had questioned his authority. For a moment, I was afraid I had placed myself in a position of danger for showing so much concern. I had not stopped to think he might suspect me; his statement had merely drawn from me genuine interest.

"And what I said is true, every word. And while I'm educating you, I'll tell you something: you know the Jews have always caused us a lot of trouble. Do you know that most of the shops and factories in Poland were owned by Jews?" He turned abruptly to his wife. "Did you know that, honey?"

She said, "No, I didn't know that. I knew they had a lot of shops . . . but . . . well, I can tell you I didn't know they owned all those factories. I thought that most of the large factories were in gentile hands."

"It does not seem to be so. Many of the largest textile factories were owned by Jews. All this time the Jews complained of being so poor. Well, let me tell you, they were richer than most gentiles. And to tell you the truth, they didn't know how to appreciate it. That's right. And it's all at our expense. That's right. Here we are, renting a Jewish farm from the German government. And it's what we deserve for ourselves. We should be owning this farm not renting it. And maybe after this war things will be put right, now that the Jews are gone."

This sort of talk I had not expected from Mr. Padworski. He seemed nervous and I figured he was upset that Mr. Shiff's sons were on the loose. My mind drifted and I thought of the Mr. Hershel I had stayed with while attending *Cheder* in Dukla. I don't know why I thought of these two men in relation to each other; perhaps, because the one thing they had in common was that they were both dead.

Mr. Padworski worried me and I shot him a glance. Generally, he was much like a kindly father to me. But I didn't want to anger him. My life was very precarious, balanced on the fine word of a lie, and should he ever discover me, I had little doubt as to the outcome.

The following day the order came through from the Germans: find the escaped Jews. The *soltys*, or mayor, set up posses for house-to-house searches and required one male from each household in Biesnik. The Padworskis sent me: and I, a Jew, ended up searching for other Jews who were no more fugitives than myself.

In groups of two and four we searched houses, sheds, and cellars for the escapees. Constantly, I prayed none would be found. I thought up a plan whereby I might save any I happened to see. At the same time I joked nervously with my fellow-searchers, solidifying my identity as a mere peasant by appearing to eagerly participate in the search.

Much to my relief the fugitives were not found. I returned to the Padworski farm late at night and was a little surprised to see the lantern lit in the kitchen. A warm feeling filled me at the thought that someone had waited up, mitigated only by the knowledge that I was deceiving them. Eager to see who was waiting up (and knowing it was probably Mrs. Padworski — her husband was always careful to delegate to himself responsibility for a good night's sleep), I burst through the kitchen door. Mr. Padworski was sitting at the table. His wife was sitting across from him and both looked rather frightened. As the door slammed shut behind me, an arm circled my throat and snapped tight. Then I was thrown against the table, and with a cry Mrs. Padworski caught me and held me to her.

"Well, well," said a voice in Yiddish. I turned around. There were two men standing by the kitchen door. Both carried sticks. I assumed they were the sons of Mr. Shiff. To make matters worse, I recognized them as men I'd seen in the market place before the war.

"Isn't this Aron's son?" said the one man to the other. The man spoken to looked me up and down, hitting his club on his hand. "Oh, it can't be . . . "

"Yes, I think it is!"

The Padworskis didn't understand Yiddish. But at any moment the brothers might direct a question to me and I panicked, winking desperately.

(In my mind raced the following scenario: 'Why did they speak to you?' said Mr. Padworski.

'I don't know why they should do such a thing. I don't know what they wanted.'

'Why did they seem to assume you would understand their language?')

"Wait," said one of the brothers. In Polish he continued: "We are going outside to look for guns we have buried. The boy we will take with us. If you make a move to resist, we will kill him."

Mrs. Padworski made a strangled noise in her throat. She released me and I went outside with the two Jews.

"Are you Aron's son?"

"Yes. Please don't give me away. They think I am a peasant boy."

The brothers laughed as if they thought it was a great joke against the Poles.

"Then I am not so upset some *goy* got my father's farm," said one of them. "They trick a Jew and a Jew tricks them."

"Laugh all you want," said his brother, "but we are still fugitives."

"That's right." The man turned to me. "Will you help us escape? We have to get some guns from the house. Then we will go and not give you away."

"Sure. I will do what I can."

At different spots around the barn they uncovered tin cans with money in them that they had hidden before they were driven out of their homes. Then we all went back to the house. They shoved me inside. The Padworskis were still at the table. Mrs. Padworski once more clutched me and I looked appropriately upset at the treatment I had received at the hands of the Jews. The brothers pried loose a board along the ceiling and removed two revolvers. Then they pointed the guns at us and laughed at the Padworski's terror.

"Take good care of our farm; we will want it back when the Nazis are destroyed," muttered one of the brothers. They demanded food. I offered to get the food and they made the Padworskis remain seated at the table. Taking them onto the back porch, I gave them all the potatoes I could find. They thanked me and I wished them well, then they took off. Mr. Padworski lamented that I had given them everything, instead of just the food that was readily visible. But Mrs. Padworski came to my defense. The night had been so frightening to both of them that they were only too glad to be safe and not worry too much about a potato-less diet for the next few days.

* * * * *

As Christmas approached Mr. Padworski reminded me he wanted to see my mother so he could work out the arrangements of my employment. For several months I had been working for room and board. This I assured him was all right with me. But I had portrayed my mother as a very poor person and Mr. Padworski naturally assumed she would be interested in some money. Of course, this presented a problem for me: how was I to present a mother I didn't have?

Mr. Padworski said, "Jusek, it's time for you to go and get your mother and bring her here to the house so we can negotiate. Remember, we said we would do this at Christmas time?"

For months he had been hinting he would like to see my mother. Although I didn't know what I could do about it, I was afraid if I stalled much longer, his suspicion would be aroused.

"O.K.," I said. "I'll do this thing."

"I'll tell you what. You can spend Christmas Eve with us and share with us the Eucharist. The next morning you can go to mass if you want, then you can pack your clothes. We will give you some presents to take to your mother and after Christmas you can bring her here and we can decide on the amount of salary she wants for your work. We are very satisfied with you. You are doing a good job and you can tell your mother we think you are a good boy."

Laughing, I said, "Thank you."

Mrs. Padworski said, "Does your mother bake *paska* (Christmas cake)?"

"No. Not this year. She . . . I don't think she will have enough flour and sugar to make *paska*."

"All right then, we'll give you some to take home to her. By the way, I forgot to ask: do you have any brothers or sisters?"

"Oh yes, sure," I said, having to think fast. "I have a sister called Sofia and, uh, a brother called, uh, called . . . Staszek."

"How old are they?"

"Oh, my sister is older and my brother is younger."

"How old is your sister?"

"Oh, she is now about fifteen, I guess, and my brother is ten."

"What does your sister do?"

"She's employed as a housemaid at a wealthy farmer's inn in Lyrzna."

"How about your brother?"

"He stays with my mother."

"Uh-huh."

In private moments behind the barn or out in the field, I was almost feverish over the meaning of the 'Uh-huh.' Every word the Padworskis said I had to analyze for any possible threat and that particular response to the explanations concerning my family did not fit comfortably in the categories I marked as safe. What if the Padworskis knew someone in Lyrżna who could report on the existence of a family named Polewski? What if someone said, "I have never met this Jusek Polewski or Sofia or Staszek. This Jusek must be fooling you." My imaginations of Gestapo brutality were strengthened and I began to wish I had run away from the Padworski farm a long time ago. I made funny remarks to Mr. Padworski and joked with him just to see if he felt friendly towards me.

On Christmas Eve, Eucharist was placed on the table. This I had never had before and I was therefore ignorant of the religious meaning. I was used to sitting in various parts of the kitchen for breakfast, lunch, and dinner. But now the occasion was special and the Padworskis sat beside me. Mr. Padworski handed me the Eucharist and said something over it. Not knowing what to do, I tried to copy him. He looked at me and said, "Don't you know what that is?"

"Sure. It looks like, like a cookie."

"Didn't you have Eucharist before in your home?"

"Yes, of course we did. But it looked different. I didn't recognize it."

Taking a piece, I ate it with them.

"Are you going to go to mass tomorrow?"

"Yes."

"Fine, then. You only go if you want to. You don't have to go. I don't go to church very often, you know. But you better go. We wouldn't want your mother to think we were trying to make a Jew out of you by not letting you go to church."

"Oh, O.K., I'll go to church tomorrow. I like to go to church. My friend Jusek — "

"That kid who stole my knife is your friend?"

"Well, he does seem like a nice boy," I said. "When I am on the pasture with the cows he often comes out with me and we play and talk a little."

Mr. Padworski said, "I hope you don't play too much and let the cows get into the oats and barley instead of being in the pasture."

"I watch the cows very carefully. I have them trained. All I do is call out a name and that cow immediately knows I want it to turn around and go in another direction."

He seemed to think this very funny. After he stopped laughing he said, "So you're going to church with Jusek the knife-stealer?" He winked and I felt a little more confident.

"Sure I am."

"Fine."

As we walked into church the next day, I was petrified. Not having the slightest idea what to do in church, I copied every move of Jusek, the knife-stealer. When he made the sign of the cross and kneeled down, I did the same. When he went over to a particular section of the church and prayed for a long time, I also did. Every now and then, I cast glances over my shoulder. No one seemed to notice that I didn't know what to do. I felt as conspicuous as someone with a big sign 'JEW' on his back, but no one seemed to be aware of me. When I finally walked back out of the church and into the bright sunshine, the breath of relief escaped my lips.

"What's the matter?" demanded my friend Jusek.

"Churches make me nervous," I blurted out. Then, in an afterthought, I added: "I have a lot of sin, you know, and it takes a long time to get it off my chest."

"Yeah," said Jusek, with a slight smirk. He swaggered a little. "I know what you mean."

* * * * *

When I got back to the house, Mrs. Padworski had soup on the table. As I sat down to eat, my mind was spinning wildly with ideas. I thought of Balvina. For some reason I had used the name of her son as my brother and maybe she could help me out. I didn't want to place her in danger; but I had to do something and it seemed I had no one else to turn to.

Suddenly, Mr. Padworski's voice cut through my thoughts.

"Jusek, you didn't tell me you were a Jew!"

My heart flew up into my throat and nearly strangled me.

"Wha — —?"

He said, "You have your hat on your head and the only people I know who wear hats on their heads in a house while they eat are Jews. So you must be a Jew!"

Panic raced through my body. I forced myself to look at him as casually as possible and noticed he was grinning, as if he'd made a joke. Slowly, my body relaxed. My eyelid twitched a little. "Of course I'm no Jew," I mumbled. Then I said, "You scared me. I thought a real Jew was in the house. You shouldn't joke around like that and call someone a Jew."

"No," he commiserated. "That's nothing to laugh about."

But he was still grinning. I lowered my eyes to the soup bowl. Some lice were swimming in it. During the war, soap was hard to find and people therefore didn't wash very often. Lice infested everything and when I took off my cap some must have fallen out of my hair.

* * * * *

In an old leather satchel my clothes were packed. The Padworskis stood on the porch together, their breath making clouds in the air around their mouths and nostrils. They waved goodbye and I waved back. Mr. Padworski had said I could use his horse for the journey and as I sat on the hard wooden seat holding the reins the cold wind made my face numb. I had on a ragged but very thick coat and around my neck was a scarf of Mrs. Padworski. The ruts in the road were frozen solid and the cart skidded along like a sled. For the rest of the afternoon, I traveled in the direction of Lyrżna. Not until darkness fell and I was sure no one would see me did I turn back.

When I arrived at the home of Balwina, the good peasant woman who lived in Bystra, it was very late. I knocked on the door. After a while it opened a crack, then opened wide.

"What are you doing here?" said Balwina. "It's so nice to see you."

She embraced me smiling warmly.

"I'm glad to see you, too."

"Well, here," she said. "Don't stand out in the cold. Come on in." She led me to a chair. Then she turned up the lamp she had evidently lit when she had risen from bed. "Who is it?" said a man's voice through the open doorway of the bedroom.

"It's nothing. No one in particular. Go back to sleep," said Balwina.

"You know," I said, "I'm working as a *pastuch* for the Padworskis in Biesnik. They live at the old Shiff farm and they treat me very well."

"Oh, I'm so glad, so glad. Do you have a different name? Oh yes, that's right, you do. The name we gave you here, 'Jusek Polewski'."

"That's right. Jusek."

"And let me look at you. You've gained weight!"

"Yes, I guess I have. That Mrs. Padworski is a very good cook."

"But what are you doing here?"

"Well, I told them I had a mother and they told me to go and get her so that money negotiations could be made. You know, negotiations about how much I was to be paid and all that. So I thought I'd just come here and spend the night, if you will let me please, and then tomorrow morning return and tell them my mother's sick and can't come to Biesnik and, you know, make up some sort of excuse."

"O.K., that sounds like a good idea," said Balwina. "You're welcome to stay here, but things are very dangerous around here as you know. There is my neighbor, Bujak, whom I don't trust. Then there is that traitor Krupa who lives not far away. You see his house in the distance," and she pointed to a nearby valley. "He told me just the other day that he had caught a Jew and delivered him to the Gestapo, for which he received a pair of boots and three thousand *zlotys*.

"Is that right? I didn't know a Jew was caught around here."

"Yes. Krupa is a real traitor to his fellow human beings. In fact, I'm surprised you didn't hear of the Jew he caught. It seems this Jew was the son of man named Shiff, who I think is the one that owned the farm you are working on. I think it is the same Shiff. There were two brothers, weren't there?"

I was stunned. After a long silence, I said quietly, "Yes."

"Well, it's the same Shiff then. Because this Jew that Krupa caught had a brother. This Krupa is a very mean person. He has been known to rape young Jewish girls. He has broken the legs of old women and dragged them to the Gestapo. And he must have done some things to that Jewish man because he learned he had a brother who was a lover to some local girl. For some extra money, he told this to the Germans.

"This girl was a peasant girl named Polka. She lives just down the road. The Germans found this Jewish lover in her house and shot him right there in front of her. The house had a dirt floor and she was forced to dig a hole right there and bury him. She pleaded to be able to bury him somewhere else, but the Germans said he was her lover, and since she liked Jews so much she might as well bury him there so he would always be with her and she wouldn't forget him."

"But how do you know all this?" I whispered, thinking of the night I had helped the Herman brothers by giving them all the potatoes I could find.

"This Krupa was sure to tell me the whole story. He had found out from some German friend, I think, or maybe he was with the Germans at the time. It's all the same. And he can't stop bragging about it, you know. He's pretty dumb. And let me tell you, someday the war's going to end and he better hope the Germans win because if they don't, someone's for sure going to take care of him. Take care of him good."

"Well, I hope so. Why does he do such things? Doesn't he have any feelings for the human race?"

"I guess he doesn't. I guess the war is not so good for lots of reasons."

We went to bed. My place was in the attic where I had stayed the last time I was in Balwina's house. In the morning Balwina insisted I take Staszek back to Biesnik with me (the two villages were not very far apart and it would be a simple matter for him to return). So I returned to the Padworskis and told them my mother was very sick and couldn't come to see them. Then I introduced Staszek to them. It just so happened Staszek and I looked very much alike, and the Padworskis believed he was my brother. I had coached him well and he supported my identity. When it was time for him to leave, Mr. Padworski offered to drive him to Lyrżna by horse and cart, but Staszek insisted he wanted to hitchhike. As if on cue, the cold weather broke and there was a day of warm breezes. Staszek left the Padworski farm and hitchhiked "home," and I was thankful to God for the warm weather because I hated to think what would have happened if the cold weather had held and Mr. Padworski thought it was too dangerous for an eleven year old boy to be hitchhiking in such temperatures.

Mr. Padworski seemed satisfied having met my pretended brother. Negotiations with my mother were put off. Staszek's visit gave me some peace of mind in that my made-up identity was reinforced; but as it turned out, my euphoria was to be short-lived. The very day that Staszek left the farm, I was working with the horse, which was a little skittery that day, and it kicked me in the thigh. Things would not have been so bad had not Mrs. Padworski insisted on seeing the wound. She wanted to see the swelling. We were in the barn where the accident happened, and *Gospondyni* (mistress of the house), as I sometimes called her, pushed me gently against the side of the stall insisting she take a look. If she pulled down my pants to see the wound, my circumcision would be in plain sight. Desperately, I twisted my head toward the barn door. "Someone's coming!" I hissed. Mrs. Padworski quickly ran to see. "Oh," she said, turning around and facing me. "There's no one coming. You're just shy!" I admitted this was true and she believed me.

During the next few months I worked very hard. Mr. Padworski still wanted to negotiate with my mother and I managed to put him off. As spring turned into summer, Staszek showed up at the farm every now and then to tell me my 'mother' was still sick and give me a report on her progress. Sometimes he would say she wanted to see me and in this way I managed to get away from the farm and spend some time playing with Staszek in the fields and woods. Mrs. Padworski would sometimes ask Staszek how my mother was doing. I had coached him very well. Mostly, he spoke only when spoken to.

One of the things that Staszek and I used to do when we got away from the Padworski farm, purportedly on the way to see my non-existent mother, was to look up some peasant girls that Staszek knew in the remote corner of Bystra, a mountainous village. We both had certain sexual feelings, and we would invite the girls outside their thatched roof log cabins into the nearby forests and attempt to feel their naked pubic areas under their long skirts. Often it resulted in the girls protesting this forward act on our part, and they would start to run in a flirtatious manner. We would catch up with them, wrestling them to the ground, and lie on top of them in a fleeting moment while we planted kisses on their lips and cheeks. I was still too young to have sexual intercourse; but during those few moments of games in the forests and fields I was able to forget about the state of war, if only for a short while.

One night I had a dream. My mother, who had died when I was a small boy, appeared and warned me I would be betrayed by Balwina. And there was some logic to this dream, for the peasant woman could very easily have gone to the Gestapo and told them about me. She could have been forced. Or she could have done it for three thousand *zlotys*. Or Staszek or Sofia could have had a slip of the tongue.

All of a sudden I realized how vulnerable I was to Balwina and became very frightened. The Germans required a daily milk delivery from the peasants with cows and it was one of my duties at the farm to take this milk to the adjacent village of Ropa. It just so happened Staszek made milk deliveries from Bystra, and while I was in Ropa we met. "Do me a favor," I said, "and tell your mother I am leaving the village of Biesnik."

Two days later I was in Ropa with another milk delivery. I tried to look out for Staszek so I could avoid him; but as I happened to turn around one time, there he was around the corner of a building, waving for me to join him. Reluctantly, I walked to where he was standing. "It's too dangerous anywhere else," he said, urgently. "You are already settled here. You have been here over a year and it's safe for you. Mother says you must not go away. You musn't run away from here."

What he said was true. Anywhere else my life would be in more danger than it was now; and Balwina could have caused me harm a long time ago had she wanted. She had, in fact, done much to help me and I decided to remain with the Padworskis in Biesnik. But I was doubly careful not to expose myself, never to bathe in public or go into the river with the other kids. Even when I played certain games with the peasant girls I was very careful. I pretended to be anti-Semitic and the big lie helped me survive. I had all kinds of prepared statements for various occasions that I felt would reinforce my position as an absolute gentile.

Life went on as usual in Poland but the war had brought on many changes. Among other things the government was in German hands and therefore reflected the interests and concerns of the Third Reich. Many Polish aspects of the government suffered from this and the mail system, for one, was unreliable.

One morning I was in the Padworskis' kitchen having soup for breakfast. Mrs. Padworski was reading a letter written by a friend of hers living in Warsaw. Tears leaked from the corners of her eyes and rand down her cheeks.

"What is the matter?" said her husband, looking at her over the top of his newspaper.

"It's what my friend here has to say about the Warsaw ghetto." She stopped, unable to continue talking, and leaned her forehead against her hand.

"What's the matter?" I said. "I would like to know about the Warsaw ghetto. They had lots of . . . Jews . . . there, didn't they?"

Mr. Padworski smiled at me. Over the past few months I had begun to think of his eyes as less cold. Behind all his Polish aristocratic bluster and anti-Semitic utterances, he was a kind, humanitarian person. I would not go so far as to reveal to him that I was Jewish, but I was no longer certain that he would be hostile if he knew.

It was he who kept me informed of the state of the German army. His various newspapers provided a steady stream of information. He seemed able to read between the lines and frequently chuckled at Germany's "minor setbacks."

His wife was evidently still thinking about the letter. In a gentle voice Mr. Padworski gave me a brief history of the Warsaw ghetto.

"In 1940 the Nazis turned part of Warsaw into an area for Jews. Around this area they put barbed wire, solid walls, and watchtowers. Jews are used to living close together but the Nazis were inhumane about it and literally piled the Jews up on top of each other. In 1942, late July I believe, this Jewish area was evacuated. That is, about three hundred thousand people went to death camps and about seventy thousand went into forced labor in the war factories."

"How do you know all this?"

"I read a lot. I talk to people. There are ways of finding out." He sighed. "Do you want to hear the rest?"

I nodded, trying not to look as upset as I felt. Visions of my previous life — the one I had spent as Shmulek Oliner — were awakening and reeling through my mind. No, I did not want to hear the rest but I was afraid to reveal my weakness.

"On April 19, 1943, the Nazis undertook the final solution of the small number of people remaining in the ghetto. General J. Stroop, commander of the ghetto operations, was there. The Jews were slaughtered like so many sheep."

"But the Germans found out something they didn't expect: not all of the Jews were sheep. They took up arms and it took the Germans three weeks to break the resistance. A few Jews escaped through the sewers, tunnels, and rat-infested Warsaw canals, and fugitives were shot down everywhere in Warsaw. I'm afraid some Polish hostages were killed as well. The Germans have a rule, you know: for every German killed here, one hundred Polish people must die. And it usually doesn't matter whether it's a Jew or a peasant that killed the German."

He might have continued but his wife gave a little sob. She smiled and brushed the tears from her cheek. "Would you like to read the letter out loud?" said her husband. Her chin crumpled a little at the suggestion but she picked up the letter.

She read: " 'Here I stand on the balcony and the entire Jewish ghetto is aflame. Dive bombers are attacking it, cannon are blasting, and tanks are moving into the ghetto. Poor devils, they haven't got the slightest chance to survive. All you see is flames and the smell of human flesh which comes from that part of the city.' " She paused and looked at her husband. "The vision of it all, why . . . it just makes me feel so sorry for those poor people. They were just people, you know, with their hatreds and loves . . . their children . . . just like us. They do fight very bravely," she said.

"In removing the Jews and making Poland *Judenrein*, Germany did us a great favor," said Mr. Padworski. I felt horrible, as if I were about to burst into a million pieces. 'Why did he have to say that again — especially now?' I thought.

"Do you really believe that?" said his wife.

After a long pause he spoke. His head was bowed. "No. No, I guess I don't. But those feelings are left unsaid."

Everyone seemed satisfied with that answer.

Except me. Yet, I also felt proud that the helpless, defenseless Jews of the Warsaw ghetto took up arms and fought back. No more can they be thought of by ignorant men as spineless sheep. After all, they were the very first people to start an armed conflict against the mighty Nazi machine in all of Europe. They killed many German soldiers in the battle of the Warsaw ghetto. It took S.S. General Jurgen Stroop, a 48 year old veteran of campaigns in Poland and Russia, an armored battalion, a cavalry battalion, a German Police battalion, Ukrainian and Polish Police squads, Latvian and Lithuanian Police units, artillery, engineers and demolition squads — in all, a 9,000 man force. Against that might the Jews had far less than a thousand young, inexperienced men, women and children who only had a few hundred revolvers, a few rifles and a few grenades, and lots of courage.

THEIR JUST DESERTS

The heavy guns of the Soviet army began to roar about forty-six kilometers away. It sounded as though the Russians were in the next village. From pulpits all over the country the "good news" was announced. The air seemed brighter, sharp and fresh, like the thaw after a long winter ice. On Sunday, the peasants flocked to their village churches filling the buildings with happy voices. And it was on Sunday the sheriff came back from the county seat of a city called Szalowa with the order given him by the Nazis to get one man out of every house to go and dig trenches in the Strurzna area. The Germans were preparing for retreat and building lines of defense every one-hundred kilometers or so.

Naturally, the Padworskis sent me. I would be living in Strurzna until the project was completed. As I was leaving the farm, *Gospondyni* gave me some sandwiches and I joined the rest of the Biesnik men and boys for the long march.

It was autumn and snow began to fall. The snow collected on the soles of my wooden shoes and I felt as if I were walking with a giant tree stump on each foot. My feet hurt. But wooden shoes were better than no shoes at all, and indeed, most of the men and boys were barefoot.

All day we walked and finally drew near the Strurzna area. An old familiar feeling came over me: like the time I went to Dukla with my sister Faye, like the time I rode in the wagon with my family to Bobowa . . . I was delivering myself into the hands of the Germans.

And strangely enough — I wasn't afraid. One possible reason was that by this time I was a veteran of trickery. Perhaps I was a bit smug in this, for as a boy of fourteen I had fooled the German army. The Germans viewed all Jews as one creature, to be shot as one and put in one grave. According to this reasoning, when they killed one Jew they killed us all.

Likewise, for me to have victory over a few Germans was to outsmart the entire Master Race. This Master Race wasn't as infallible as it had wished to seem. Lines of retreat were being formed and I reveled in the power of the Western Allies. My dreams of England, America, and Russia coming to the rescue, once dashed when Balwina confirmed the death of my family, were renewed. I looked on the Germans as vicious dogs with their teeth pulled out. Inasmuch as the Allies were winning the war, I myself was victorious, and I swaggered just a little on that last stretch of road before Strurzna.

As we walked in single file through the gates, we were told to stand at attention while our names were called out. This was to determine whether anyone had run away. I heard my name called, "Jusek Polewski," and said, "Here!" The officer gave me a look and his face seemed very ugly. I thought how that face would look to the Russians with fear all over it. He finished reading the list and showed us to the barracks which were small wooden huts built of one-inch boards.

I was taken away from my Biesnik neighbors and put with a group of boys my own age, one of whom I immediately distrusted. He reminded me of the "knife stealer." The guard pointed to a spot on the floor and told me that was where I would sleep. It had been the "bunk" of a boy who ran away from the barracks during an air raid. On this spot I spread the coarse blanket Mrs. Padworski had given me. A whistle sounded and I took my tin cup to the mess area for some soup. After the cold walk to Strurzna I was more than happy to drink something warm. After the soup I went back to the barracks to get some sleep.

The other boys back in the barracks looked tired and rather vicious. They said they had worked there four days and that the German detail boss was a real devil. He would come around by jeep every hour of the day and beat those who didn't work hard enough. If any of the peasants would say anything, the German answered, "Die you devil." In fact, the peasants had nicknamed him, *Zdechipieronie,* or, "Die You Devil."

That night I didn't sleep very well. Most of the time I lay waiting for dawn. Then we got up and received soup and a piece of dry army bread.

All too soon the work started. The fields marked off for trenches had been sown with winter corn. A truck appeared with spades and picks and each of us took a tool and started to work. The only clothing I had on was a pair of pants, a homespun shirt and an old jacket Mr. Padworski had given me. Of course, I had no underclothing, and the wind made my skin feel like ice. We dug in the frozen ground until twelve o'clock and then a whistle blew for a half-hour lunch break. I had saved the sandwich Mrs. Padworski had given me. It was dry and hard but I was so hungry it tasted absolutely delicious.

At six-thirty in the evening we went back to the barracks. I was dead tired and slept soundly in spite of the cold. The next day passed the same as the first. We dug in the frozen ground all morning and had a short lunch break. At six-thirty the whistle blew for us to stop work.

Strurzna was an important railroad junction and some German military trains were stopped there. Some of the cars were being unloaded into open wagons. Other cars were being filled up with food for the German army. We were marching by the railway station on the way back to the barracks when two "sisters" — small Russian planes that harassed the German military lines — appeared very swiftly from beyond the horizon and machine-gunned the Strurzna station. We all jumped into the trenches we had dug the previous day. More planes arrived and then the real fire opened up. Bullets hit so close we could hear them whistle by our heads. The roar of the diving planes was deafening. The train started out quickly and the two sister planes followed it, diving and machine-gunning the box cars. Pretty soon whistles blew and we climbed out of the trenches and resumed the march back to the barracks.

After dinner, which was more soup and bread, I returned to the barracks with the other boys. There was not much light inside the building. In the light of a candle everyone knelt down to say prayers. Everyone spoke loud enough for his neighbor to hear and I did the same. It just so happened that the boy who reminded me of the "knife stealer" was beside me on the floor and apparently my prayer was not to his liking.

He said, "Hey, everybody knows how to pray. Only Jews don't know how to pray to Jesus Christ."

He seemed to be talking to me, so I said, "Sure, that's right."

"Are you a Jew?"

I grew pale from the sudden shock. Very quickly I said, "Yeah. You're a Jew too, aren't you?"

"No, I'm not. Hey fellas, we got us a Jew boy."

He laughed and waited to see what I would do.

"Oh yeah, fellas," I said. "We got two Jews among us. Don't you see? Doesn't he look like a Jew?"

The boy walked over and pushed me. I pushed him back. Then he hit me and I hit him in the eye as hard as I could and just then the guard walked by the window and saw the scuffle. He opened the door and said, "What's going on here!"

"Here is a Jew, that's what. I caught him right here in the barracks."

The guard shot me a searching glance. Mostly though, he seemed irritated at all the commotion.

"Here is a Jew," the boy repeated his accusation, pointing his finger at me.

Right there in front of me I saw death, and the guard said:

"It's too dark in here now. Tomorrow I'll take a look at him."

After the guard left the boy was surly. He said, "Don't tell me, Jusek, your mother never taught you the *paczierz* (the prayer)?" Then he kidded: "Maybe you are a Jew. I heard last week a Jew escaped and maybe you are that guy."

"Oh sure. Sure, I'm that guy."

My heart was beating so hard I thought that everyone should be able to hear it. At any moment I could be delivered into German hands. I pretended to laugh at the other boy and he got up and walked toward the door, apparently to go to the bathroom.

"Gee," he said, "I better leave here. I don't want to share these barracks with a Jew."

That night I lay on the hard floor with the rough blanket on my shoulder and sleep seemed as far away as the Free World. If the guard inspected me in the morning he would plainly see I was a Jew. I really didn't want to fall asleep because that would only make the morning come faster. I was very upset and prayed to God over and over again, trying to think of what to do.

Then I remembered a conversation I had overheard the previous day. Two peasant men were planning to run away. They had commented that the Germans didn't keep very good track of the workers; the records were not kept up to date and the only thing a person had to be concerned about was getting shot in the actual effort of the escape. In my own case, I had responded to roll call and I was sure if some German guard noticed I was missing he would think I had been transferred to another work team or something. Until nearly daylight I made plans and all kinds of fantasies filled my head; all kinds of possible escapes and the tortures and deaths in store if I failed.

Sometime toward dawn I dozed and in a dream my mother appeared to me. Very clearly, she sat by the bed and whispered in my ear, telling me to take a certain route of escape down by the river that flowed near the place where we were digging trenches. In the dream I ran and ran, crossing a river and running on. My mother, who had died of tuberculosis, ran with me. Then we were standing on a nice lawn. The sun was shining and there was a pleasant smell in the air.

When the whistle blew for us to wake up and everyone crawled grumbling out of bed, I decided I had better do something about my prayer. There were about six words I knew and I got on my knees and said each word very loudly. The Polish boys turned and looked at me and one of them said, "He's no Jew. See? He knows the prayer well enough."

When I had recited the prayer twice through to make sure everyone had a chance to hear, I went over to the boy I had fought with the night before and apologized. "I'm sorry we had that fight," I said. "We should not be arguing and fighting. We have a hard days work ahead of us." He turned so I could plainly see his black and swollen eye and walked away without speaking to me.

All this time I was aware the guard might come into the barracks without a moments warning and have me take my pants down. It would be all over then. Every time the barracks door shuddered on its hinges — as it did quite often because of the wind that had arrived in the night — I would hold my breath. After having lived in a state of fear for years, I thought I would have been used to the strain. But when the likelihood of losing my life seemed so great and the very next minute might very well be my last, my head filled with noises like a bag full of drowning cats. The guard had said he would check me. And all the pain and trickery of the past few months seemed for nothing. What difference did it make when I died, if the choices of time were only a few months apart? I might as well have been with my family; and why was I allowed to hope and dream and fight for the impossible? The end of the war was near. Russian bombers flew regular missions across Nazi territory. Why was I allowed to survive the worst only to perish when the Allies were knocking at the door?

Then the bombing started. The barracks shook and sawdust fell from the cracks in the ceiling. There was mass confusion and the workers flopped on the floor, some whimpering and others just very quiet. I was lying next to the "knife stealer"and for the moment we were comrades, both afflicted by death and forgetting the differences between us.

The bombing stopped suddenly and the sound of planes disappeared into the distance. How small these sounds were — — how profound the stillness — — when compared to the crashing explosions of bombs! The boys got up from the floor murmuring and trying to tell jokes. Those who had whimpered and cried laughed nervously trying to pass it off. I was wiping sawdust from my pants, feeling great relief that the bombing was over, when the door opened and the German guard walked in.

I snapped erect and the blood left my head so quickly I nearly fainted. He looked right at me and I wished I had died in the bombing raid. "Everyone out!" he said. "Out in formation!" My knees were weak and my stomach moved up into my throat. I thought, 'He is just playing with me. Maybe I should start running and get shot running.' While we marched in formation he looked at me again. His face was cold and ugly, hard as metal, and I was sure he was playing with me, waiting perhaps until I died of fright. The wooden shoes had made large blisters on my feet and I limped a little. All the while, I acted brave and stupid, like the German boys I saw from time to time, pretending, ironically, my race was the chosen of God. I wished it were yesterday all over again; or tomorrow or a year from now, with everything done.

As we passed the Strurzna junction the guards ordered us to look straight ahead. The bombing raid had resulted in masses of bodies, shattered arms and legs, torn bellies, and blood all over the place. The Germans ordered us not to look to the left or right, but to keep our eyes straight ahead as we marched past the station. The moans were sickening and I felt devilish joy that the Master Race was so human after all. Not only were the Nazis losing the war, they were lying dead at my feet. They died with pleas for mercy on their lips. With calls to God they passed into death and I felt somehow Zyndranowa and Bielanka and countless Jews were getting their revenge.

We were digging in the trenches when the second bombing raid occurred. The planes came one after another, dropping bombs, and the ground heaved and shook and quivered. From the direction of the train, ghastly human screams split the air only to be cut off in the explosions. The station was a shambles. One of the airplanes spun around in the air and came over so low above the trenches that I could see the grim expression on the pilot's face. 'This is the end,' I thought. 'Now I will be machine-gunned by a Russian plane.' The air turbulence from the plane passing overhead flapped my hair about. The deafening roar of the engine seemed to draw from me a similar long and hideous sound and I lay shaking in the jagged icy bottom of the trench.

After about twenty minutes of bombing the planes flew away. Silence descended like a deafness over the trenches. The cries and moans of wounded men, mostly Germans, sounded far away and a little unreal. Smoke filled the air and fire licked and hissed among the ruins of the Strurzna station. It seemed impossible that I was still alive. Like a phantom I rose from the ground and was appalled at the death and destruction strewn everywhere. Deep inside me was a satisfaction that it was the Germans who had suffered most in this ordeal. Secretly I applauded because the Germans were finally getting what they deserved.

A whistle blew and we were ordered to resume working. Some of the work force had been killed and other members had to carry the bodies off a little ways to the edge of the woods. It started to rain. What clothes I had on were wet to the skin and the Germans walked about in shiny black slickers, bending over with water dripping from their helmets and taking care of their dead and wounded comrades. My wooden shoes filled with water. The ground was softening to icy mud and my shoes stuck in the mud and came off. From time to time I fell. The mud felt cold and gritty against my back and belly. The trenches were filling with water and we had to dig and splash with the pick in the muddy slosh. The German guard seemed to keep his eye on me. I was sure he knew I was a Jew and that he would want to take a look at me back at the barracks. Or maybe at the end of the cold miserable day he would shoot me and let me die in this muddy water.

The rain came down even more heavily and we ran to the woods for shelter. The guards kept a close eye on everyone. The two peasants I had overheard planning to escape took their break for freedom, running hunched low through the trees and wiry underbrush. One of the guards sounded the alarm and another guard several meters deeper in the woods shot five times and both peasants were dead in their tracks. From where I was taking shelter under a stubby evergreen tree I could see the bodies lying washed by the rain.

Escape seemed impossible and fear made a funny taste in my mouth. The rain let up a little and Russian bombers made another pass at the Strurzna station. The Germans were transporting men from the Russian front to Italy, and the Russians bombed the transport lines again and again. As fast as the Germans could lay track the Russians blew it apart again. The guards ran through the woods shouting at us to get back to the trenches.

Some of the workers did as they were told and ran as quickly as they could through the falling rain. The roar of airplane engines vibrated along the ground and the guards were firing their rifles into the air. The planes flew so low I thought I could reach out and touch them. The Germans had wild, frightened looks in their eyes. Their mouths hung open. The workers were milling about, some heading for the trenches, others just running around in circles with their hands over their ears. A peasant right in front of me spun around on his heels and collapsed on his knees. His mouth was open and I knew he was screaming, but his voice was lost in the din of plane engines. Then the bombs fell, whistling first, and the ground coughed and heaved with the explosions. In the confusion I scrambled on my hands and knees in the direction opposite to the trenches, tearing the underbrush with my hands, rolling and crawling and shoving my way through the woods.

With all the din of carnage behind me I couldn't tell if I was being shot at. It didn't seem to matter. With the wings of fear I skidded through the sodden tree leaves and rolled down a bank. Rain struck hard against every part of my body and when I came to a river I plunged right in and crossed to the other side. The bombing back at the station continued but now the explosions didn't quite drown out everything else. The distance I had come away from the trenches was in many ways comforting and now I could hear the hiss of rain falling upon the surface of the river. I imagined that back at the station the hiss was that of fire. Even at this distance I could hear an occasional bloodcurdling scream. In the dream I'd had where my mother paid me a visit there was a river like the one at my feet. The river was behind me now and, as in the dream, I knew I was safe.

Weak from lack of food I tightened in my fist the loose skin of my belly. One of my shoes was gone and I threw the other one into the river and watched it float away. My feet were so blistered that the freedom felt good in spite of the cold. Toward nightfall I knocked at a peasant's door and asked if he would put me up for the night, saying I had visited a little village past Strurzna and was on my way home. He looked me up and down and a strange sight I must have been! Suddenly aware of myself, I looked down brushing a little at my sleeve. The rain had washed the mud from my clothing. My hands were scratched and my feet were torn and blistered and bleeding. The skin of my face burned and I knew that it must have been scratched as well.

Finally the peasant said, "O.K., you can sleep in the stable."

He gave me some bread and milk which I took to the barn. The peasant let me find out for myself that I was not alone in the stable. Also sleeping there was some kind of deformed, crippled child. When I sat down in the straw to eat the bread and milk, this deformed child made strange noises. Traditionally, deformed children born to peasants were kept at home and often in some isolated place such as a stable, attic or spare room. They were fed and left alone until they died. It was my luck to share a stable with such a cripple.

When I returned to Biesnik the Padworskis greeted me warmly. Many persons from the village had escaped the labor camps in addition to myself. The Padworskis were concerned that the Germans might try to hunt down the fugitives but mostly they were just happy to see me alive.

During the short period of rest and relative peace that followed, I spent long hours thinking of the events of the past few years of my life. Everything sacred to me had been crushed. My family was dead. My heritage had made me a criminal and my will to survive had sealed my fate. If the Germans caught up with me now I would be shot, not as a Jew, but as a fugitive from the Strurzna work camp.

For some reason I recalled an incident that had happened only a week after I came to live with the Padworskis. I had found a Jewish prayer book which I hid under my pillow in the barn and used each night to help me pray. One day Mrs. Padworski found it. She said, "What is this? Where did you get it?" I said, "I just found it. I don't know what it is. I found it in a little cloth sack along the road outside of town. What is it?" She said, "Well, you better burn it because it is a Jewish book and if anyone finds it on you they will think you are a Jew."

So I said, "Oh, sure." And I burned it.

* * * * *

Not long after my escape from Strurzna I began to notice a change in the Germans who were passing through Biesnik. Their hard, cruel masks were disintegrating. Little by little they were forced to realize that the arm of the Third Reich had lost its muscle. They even began to smile, sometimes, in the nervous, ingratiating manner of defeat, and to help out the villagers. One German lent his hand to the changing of a broken cart wheel. Another helped build a chicken coop and refused to accept payment for his work. On the village streets some German soldiers greeted pleasantly the passersby and tried to engage them in conversation, doing what they could to prove they weren't so mean after all.

The air was crisp and filled with whisperings that the German army was retreating. The three-year-long dream was coming true: the Germans were taking a beating; they were being shot down like dogs by the Polish partisans. Small groups of Jewish partisans also operated in the area. Germans feared the darkness and no longer dared come out of town at night; Polish traitors who had mistreated Jewish men, women and children got diminishing support from the Master Race and were understandably less brave. I knew of a man named Lega who had turned many Jews over to the Gestapo. A Jewish partisan group operating out of a forest just outside Gorlice paid this Lega several visits and during these visits he was left with all limbs broken.

For the next few weeks the guns of the Russian liberators blasted at the enemy from Jaslo, a city about seventy kilometers away. Germans were withdrawing under the pressure. Partisans sabotaged the lines of retreat. Bridges were blown up, trees chopped down and thrown across the escape routes of the demoralized army. Russian planes strafed the roads during the day and the Germans were forced to flee by night.

It seemed only a matter of days – perhaps even hours – before the enemy would be kicked out forever from the Gorlice-Biesnik district. The future was bright and mysterious and I awakened each day with a feeling of excitement. Fear no longer seemed necessary and my chest swelled with fresh and powerful hope. With freedom so close I tried to recall the prewar days. It seemed too good to be true that I would no longer have to fear being a Jew. Once more I would be able to walk the streets openly and speak Yiddish to my people! Yet some vague notion kept my happiness from being complete. After the war was over I rather expected my life to return to the idealistic simplicity of my youth. Life had robbed me of my family so quickly I couldn't completely comprehend their death. And to a certain extent I guess I did, in fact, hold onto the hope of their survival; some small part of me held tenaciously to the hope that they were somewhere safe and sound, waiting for me – perhaps in England or America, countries which were only names to me but certainly symbolizing heaven. Some elusive but nevertheless ominous cloud threatened my shining sun, and I thought this uneasiness was due to the fact that in spite of their losses the German armies were still occupying my country – Poland.

The Germans kept saying they would push the Russians back – the sweet luscious liberators – all the way back to Russia. I could not imagine the nightmare of losing the war. Not after all the hope and reason to dream. And I held desperately to each moment those four weeks before I finally saw the Russians. During those four weeks I prayed to God that the Russians would come quickly. And when the shooting was very near with shells exploding above the roofs of Biesnik I said the longest prayer I could remember from Hebrew school.

The shells were exploding right outside Biesnik and bullets were flying everywhere. Sleep was impossible and I huddled with the Padworskis in the kitchen of their house. We sat in darkness. Not a sound did anyone make, yet clearly we knew what each one was thinking. 'What is happening? Will we make it? What does this all mean?' Life was extremely uncertain. By dawn the next day we could all be dead and there was no telling whether it would be a German or a Russian action that put us to death. Mrs. Padworski clutched me and her husband held onto both of us. At three o'clock in the morning someone came pounding on the door and with a sigh of resignation Mr. Padworski got up to open it.

Standing out on the porch was one of their neighbors. Exploding shells illuminated him and he burst into the house and took Mr. Padworski by the arm.

"The Germans are taking horses with them," he shouted. "The Russians are pushing the Germans back and they're blowing up bridges and supplies as they retreat and they're taking horses!"

The man dashed out into the night once again and Mr. Padworski took his wife and headed toward the cellar, shouting at me to save the horse.

Out in the cold blue night lit by flashes like lightning the snow was deep and frozen hard. As usual I had little to wear and the cold was bitter right down to the bone. I took the horse out of the stable. He was jumpy and I had to fight him a little in the barnyard. Rockets exploded overhead lighting up the snow on the ground. The noise made the horse wild. I kicked my heels into his ribs and succeeded in driving him in the direction of the woods.

Just when I thought I had controlled the animal and we were finally safe, a low-hanging branch swept from nowhere and knocked me off the horse's back. Strange sounds trickled through my head. My body felt dull and soggy. Strangely enough I felt no pain; the coldness of the night seemed far, far away and I came to the logical conclusion that I was dead. My mind seemed to swirl on an eddy of frozen wind and I thought: 'Here I have outsmarted the Germans as I vowed so long ago to do only to give my life to the next tree while on the back of a dumb animal.'

Then the pain started creeping up on me and there was soon no doubt that I was very much alive. My body seemed broken into a million pieces and each piece ached. Coughing and groaning aloud I got to my feet and stumbled after the horse. In the terrible light shed by rockets I found him and we waited out the night huddled together by a windfall. I held the horse around the neck and several times he stepped on my feet. As dawn made the sky pink I headed back toward the farm, my body aching stiff and numb with cold. The horse was calm now and I lay on his back; only the hope of Russian victory had kept me alive.

That morning was the morning of mornings. On such a cold miserable night as the one I had spent in the woods, a person might have wished for death. My body was tired and aching and my mind felt feverish. Mrs. Padworski clucked over me like a mother hen. She fed me bread and hot tea and insisted that I sleep in her own bed. The tea spread a blanket of warmth down my insides. As I headed toward the bedroom I just happened to glance out the window of the kitchen and what I saw made all the pain and fatigue instantly leave my body. Marching across the field in back of the barn were five men in white snow uniforms. They came from the east. I fell to my knees and said a silent agonizing prayer in Yiddish.

THE LIBERATORS

In that month of March, 1945 the Germans were pushed out of Biesnik. The Russians marched into the Padworski house and set up a radio in the bedroom. Mr. Padworski fell into a serious illness and his wife made a bed for him in the stable. He suffered from angina pectoris I was told. The Russians were constantly drunk on the vodka they carried in their canteens. They had no food supplies or extra clothes with them. They were known to live off the land, and Mrs. Padworski fed them from the larder.

My bed was also in the stable, as it had been all along. *Gospondyni* continued to sleep in the house, although she made frequent visits to the warm stable in order to attend to her husband.

"The war is nearly over," sighed Mr. Padworski, looking pleased but very tired. His bed was made up in an empty horse stall where he could have some privacy. From my own bed I couldn't see him but frequently he called me over for conversation.

"For us the war is already ended," I said. "Isn't it? The Germans are being pushed out of Poland. Biesnik already is saved by the liberators."

"The liberators . . ."

Mr. Padworski lay on his bed and stared at the ceiling. He seemed very pale. Throughout the war his friends, whom you might call the intelligentsia, had come to the farm on periodic visits. On these occasions there were reports on the progress of the war as well as philosophical discussions about war in general. Mr. Padworski felt no love toward the Germans. Neither did he seem particularly affectionate towards the Russians. His interest lay exclusively with the Polish people, and it was only tact that ever made it seem otherwise.

"Yes, the Germans have been pushed back," he said. "The Germans are gone and I am thankful. When the Russians have left us, too — then I would say the war has ended and we Poles will be truly free."

I sat on a wooden crate at the end of the stall. The barn door was open and I could see a Russian officer standing on the porch of the house. He was smoking a cigarette, blowing smoke away on the cold, crisp March air. Wood smoke was coming from the chimney of the house and every now and then someone moved past the kitchen window. Soon spring would break the grip of winter and then the vine alongside the house would bloom. The earth would be ready for planting. A whole new season would come and then go.

"It's ironic," continued Mr. Padworski. "It's ironic . . . when the war came to Poland I left the city and moved to the country. I was an engineer with a good business. But you know, I left the city because it is a bad place to be in time of war. I brought my young wife here to this Jewish farm because a farm is much safer than the city. Here, I thought, we could be safe. We could sit out the war and be sheltered and await the brighter days of the new future."

He was staring at the ceiling, speaking aloud the thoughts that ran through his head. I felt uneasy. He looked very pale lying there staring upward and he spoke as one might to a Christian priest.

"My wife is fifteen years younger than myself. She is good to me and very hard working, but we have been unable to have children of our own. I sometimes fear she is lonely."

Nervously, I coughed and got up from the wooden crate. Just then his wife walked into the stable carrying food for his lunch. Her eyes looked tired and the war had aged her until she looked as old as her husband. She sat on the wooden crate I had just left and smoothed a place in the hay so she could set down the plate of biscuits.

With hushed voice she said: "Some German army soldiers who apparently were stragglers have been captured!"

I glanced at the porch of the house and noticed the Russian officer was no longer there. Mrs. Padworski fed her husband some soup from a bowl she had carried on the plate of biscuits.

"While I was in the kitchen these two Germans were brought in. They were dirty and unshaven and looked very frightened. They looked at me pleadingly, as if for help, and Lord knows I couldn't help them. Not that I wouldn't if I could, even though they are the enemy."

Mr. Padworski murmured: "The tides of war have changed."

"And then while I was standing right there . . . well, the Russian who brought the prisoners in asked what should be done with them. I thought they would be locked up in the barn or something, maybe tied up. But the Russian officer just glanced at the prisoners and said, 'You know what to do with Germans.' Simple as that. And the Russian who had brought the prisoners in pushed them back out the door."

"Where are they now?" I said.

"In back of the barn someplace, I think. I am afraid of what's going to happen. In spite of their cruelty the Germans are real people. The Russian officer didn't seem to recognize this."

Filled with morbid curiosity, I ran outside the barn and looked around. The glare of the sun on the snow momentarily blinded me. The snow was trampled and muddy between the house and barn; there was no one in sight. I ran around the barn and stopped short.

Two Germans were on their knees in the snow at the Russian soldier's feet. With tears running down their stubbly cheeks the Germans choked: "Please, please. We have wives. We have children." With the barrel of his machine gun the Russian motioned them to their feet. "Walk on," he said in German. Desperately, the Germans glanced at each other. Once more they turned to beg and again the Russian motioned them to their feet.

Trembling, the Germans rose to their feet. Their coats had been taken away and they wore only coarse army shirts across their shoulders. Snow clung to their pant legs all the way up to the knees. Resolutely they turned around and walked away from the Russian. One of them stopped and turned back and the other waited for him. "Please . . . " The Russian said, "Walk on." The Germans resumed their walk. They assumed peculiar set expressions. As they walked, the Russian very suddenly opened fire with his machine gun and the Germans were flung face down in the snow. They struggled feebly. The snow was red with their blood and I vomited against the side of the barn. The Russian turned around and saw me. He had a certain nonchalance, and in his eyes was the coldness so closely connected with death.

"You shouldn't have seen this," he said, he face expressionless. "Go to the house. My captain wants to see you."

* * * * *

Gospondyni was in the kitchen when I walked through the door. I avoided her eyes. A pair of Russian army boots were against the wall by the door. Several white snow uniforms hung on nails newly pounded into the wall. Steam rose from a large pot of stew on the stove and from the bedroom came Russian words and the static of a radio. Throughout the war Mr. Padworski had saved his newspapers, stacking them in a corner of the kitchen. Now they were gone. Thick was the smell of gun grease and the odor of unwashed bodies. The Russian officer was seated at the table.

The Russians had demanded *Forshpun,* which simply meant they required any type of transportation Mr. Padworski had to offer. The Russian officer looked directly at me.

"You will go to the neighboring farm and get a horse. They you will hitch it to the wagon along with the horse in the barn."

I glanced at Mrs. Padworski and our eyes connected. She was usually a very expressive person and I was shocked by the lack of feeling in her gaze. In this house taken over by soldiers she evidently kept her emotions carefully guarded. Someone would have to drive the horses to the Russian front. The Russians couldn't spare soldiers for this purpose and I feared I would probably get the job. For several moments my eyes were riveted to those of *Gospondyni.* Then she turned her attention to the stew that was cooking on the stove.

When I returned from the neighboring farm with the horse, I found several Russian soldiers I had not seen before standing in the barnyard smoking cigarettes. They took periodic drinks from their canteens and I could tell they were drunk. I took the Padworskis' horse out of the barn and hitched the two horses to the wagon. One of the Russians shouted at me to put straw in the wagon bed. This I did, and some of the soldiers piled in. The officer came out onto the porch of the house. He told me to drive the wagon to the front lines where it was needed for supplies and transportation.

As I whipped up the horses and drove out of the driveway I couldn't help but glance in back of the barn. There in the red snow lay the two Germans, face down and stripped to their underwear.

* * * * *

The soldiers in the back of the wagon were wild and boisterous. Every now and then they had me drive into a farm that was close to the road and they would get off the wagon and knock on the door of the house and ask for women. All the young women were taken to the various outbuildings, and I could hear them pleading and screaming and sometimes crying. The Russians would say, "I have liberated you. Now let me have you."

Sometimes the farmers knew what the Russians were after and when they saw the wagon coming they hid their women. It was on one of these farms that a particular Russian's appetite turned from women to beef. He paid the farmer for his cow (the farmer had little choice), then took an axe from the back of the wagon and went into the barn. The cow was in its stall. The Russian led the cow out of the stall and tied it to a wooden post in the middle of the barn. Then he hit it between the eyes with the axe. The head of the axe flew off the handle and the cow fell to its knees with a terrible bellow. The cow just stayed there on its knees, bawling loudly, while the Russian searched the hay for the axe head. He finally found it and hit the cow again, and there was instant food in the evening for the soldiers. The meat was cooked in a huge cauldron.

* * * * *

Once spring finally came the weather changed quickly. The snow turned soft and very wet. The roads were at places axle deep with mud. I had to whip the horses constantly to keep them going and along the front lines where the fighting was going on I could see the whites of the horses' frightened eyes. The fighting seemed to attract dark clouds which filled the sky and rain fell steadily turning the road to a quagmire of running water. Cannon fire and machine gun fire split the air and bullets whistled close overhead. In addition to myself, there were other drivers — boys my own age from other farms — along this treacherous front. One of these drivers was killed by a stray bullet and there was no way of telling whether it was a German or a Russian who fired the shot.

The war was moving over territory previously occupied by the Germans. Crumbling in the various fields were the hollow shells and crumbling remains of farmhouses, and in spite of the danger of each breathing second, my mind would wander. I thought of my family, Isak and Reisel, my two dead mothers and my father. Desperately I held onto the hope that someone other than myself had survived somewhere, for the burden of their memory seemed too much to bear alone. The thought that I was all that was left of them made me feel wretched with lonelines and the unfairness of life.

Driving near the front I saw many cruelties. Dead German soldiers dismembered, decapitated, hung in grotesque display. I was appalled; yet also morbidly gratified. The souls of murdered Jews numbered in the tens of thousands. The more I found out from stories here and there, the more I was convinced millions of my people had perished. At this point I learned of the existence of gas chambers all over liberated Poland and Russia. And compared to this what was the mutilated body of a German soldier?

Yet as *Gospondyni* had said the Germans were people too. And I struggled with conflicting feelings of compassion and the desire for revenge.

Conflicting also were my feelings in regard to the Russians. They were not so glorious after all. The thrill of their power I felt and the joy of their victory. But those who I had previously thought of as the "sweet luscious liberators" were just the other side of a well-worn coin. War was war, soldiers were soldiers; and the Russians sometimes raped, looted, and even murdered with impunity. I was not certain they would treat me any differently than the Germans would have were they to know I was Jewish. I decided that it was not yet safe to disclose my true identity.

One night I decided I'd had enough. I was staying with a small contingent of soldiers at a newly occupied village; and in the middle of the night while the drunken revelry was still going strong, I slipped out of the room where I was staying. The moon was hidden behind clouds, the night very dark. Mr. Padworski's horse was in a barn with the other horses. The guard at the door was asleep and I led the horse quietly out the back door. All night long I rode. The country was strange and I rode in the general direction of Biesnik until I hit familiar territory.

The Padworskis were glad to see me. The Russians had moved on taking all their equipment with them, and Mr. Padworski's bed was now back in the house. He was especially pleased I had returned with the horse, for as a result of the war, horses had become extremely rare. A farmer's livelihood depended upon this beast of burden, for ploughing, etc. In addition to being practical, they were symbols of status; and Mr. Padworski now had one of the few such animals in the village.

* * * * *

One morning in early April I saw someone waving to me from a hill about half a mile in back of the barn. It looked like Staszek. I went a little closer and it was, indeed, the son of Balwina. I ran up to him and we greeted each other warmly.

He said, "You know a Jewish man by the name of Peller?"

"Sure. He's my father's friend from Moszczenica. Peller had a wife and two beautiful children."

"When the Germans were pushed away from here the Jews that were still alive came out of hiding. This Peller came to see my mother to find out if anyone in the Oliner family was alive and she told him you were alive and that you were to be found here in Biesnik. He's looking for you. That is, he wants to see you and my mother sent me to tell you that."

"I can't believe it. This is wonderful! Sure, uh, come with me. We'll — that is, I'll have to tell Mr. Padworski."

Staszek walked back to the farm with me. Mr. Padworski was recuperating from his illness and doing some light work in the barn. I told him my mother was sick again and needed me. He gave his permission for me to go and Staszek and I left immediately.

As I was walking with Staszek across the Biesnik-Bystra ridges a very peaceful, lovely, exciting feeling came over me. 'Now there is freedom for me.' I thought to myself. I greatly anticipated seeing Peller. We walked very fast. Staszek had trouble keeping up with me.

When Balwina saw me she hugged me and made the sign of the cross and cried and kissed me. "The war is over," she said. "You're safe. You don't have to be afraid anymore. I will send for a man I want you to meet."

In a short while Peller arrived. We embraced and he then told me all about how he had survived the war in a village called Moszczenica in the stable attic of a kindly peasant widow. The woman had risked her life in the hope she might convert an infidel to Christianity. Then he told me what was happening in Gorlice. Out of many thousands of Jews only about fifty remained. Peller and several other Jews lived in a large house he had managed to rent from the occupying Russians and the newly established Polish government. He urged me to live with them saying that now the war was over and it was all right to be a Jew and that in fact the Jews had to band together in order to get what was rightfully theirs: justice, freedom, and a rebuilding of their destroyed psyches.

I agreed with him. We parted and I made arrangements with Staszek to come back to the Padworski farm and help me pack. Then I returned to the Padworskis and told them my mother's illness was very serious and that she needed me nearby. Did that mean I could no longer work for the Padworskis? Yes. Leaving the farm was very painful. I had been as a son to them. Mrs. Padworski cried and gave me a gift of grain which was very valuable at that time. Mr. Padworski gave me some old clothing. He had a very strange look in his eyes when he said the final goodbye. I was beginning to wonder again if they knew my true identity. I was sure they both knew I was Jewish and I couldn't look them in the eyes. I was ashamed. Had any of the Germans found out that I was Jewish the Padworskis could have been killed. Because of me they had been in grave danger. Although Mr. Padworski had made a number of anti—semitic remarks during the three years of my service, I sometimes felt that he didn't mean them. Maybe it was just the tragedy of war that made him say those nasty things. Some truths were better left unacknowledged, given the circumstances of war, I thought to myself. But I couldn't help feeling ashamed. They had treated me like a son; and even if they intuitively knew the truth, the fact of attempted deceit was a painful barrier between us. I had lived a lie and I left the Padworski farm for the last time with tears in my eyes.

Peller was a loving, caring, self-proclaimed leader of the surviving Jews in the city of Gorlice. I lived with him a short while and during this time we spoke only Yiddish because he wanted me to remember my roots. The words rolled off my tongue strangely. Sometimes they dropped heavily to the ground, other times they soared like birds. Gradually, I got the old rhythm back. Jusek Polewski stepped aside and I was Shmulek Oliner once more. Peller became my legal guardian. He went with me to the courthouse in Gorlice and helped me reclaim the land of my grandfather in Mszanka and my father and stepmother in Bielanka, which I turned over to Balwina and her children. I never returned to Zyndranowa. Rumors circulated that Jews in that part of the country had been put into a ghetto in Dukla. One look at the land of my grandfather in Mszanka and also that of my father in Bielank convinced me I didn't want to see grandfather Isak's farm. I couldn't bear to think of that house — once so full of life — now as a hollow shell overgrown with weeds; a haunted replica of the past, with broken windows, stolen doors, and empty chimneys.

With the help of Peller I went to the Russian military authority in charge of Gorlice and requested I be notified in the event any of my relatives were discovered alive. In this way I found out that a cousin of my father's had indeed survived the war and was presently living in another part of Gorlice. Peller couldn't go with me to look up this relative so I went alone. The streets were narrow and winding, the houses all jumbled together, and I had some trouble finding where this distant cousin lived. Then I heard a woman talking rapidly, loudly and in a somewhat agitated voice. I ran a little faster into the hallway of a single dwelling which was my cousin's house and I saw a young Russian soldier inside a room in which the door was open. The woman noticed me and looked extremely relieved. She shouted, "Shmulek." She appeared to have heard about my survival from Peller. The Russian soldier saw me for the first time and mumbled something under his breath, turned and left, brushing past me. I noticed the woman was somewhat embarrassed about what might have happened had I not appeared on the scene. She immediately composed herself and embraced me saying, "You must be Aron's son, Shmulek." "Yes, I am," I said. Her husband showed up shortly. We embraced and for the first time since Bobowa I had a genuine feeling that I had a remnant of a family again. My stay and frequent visits afterwards were very pleasant. We started talking about what had happened to our families during the catastrophe. They knew of no other survivors in the Oliner family. This news was very disheartening. Nevertheless, when I left to go home that late afternoon, I felt pretty good. After all, I had found someone who was family and who cared. I felt useful and important in that I was able to prevent an unpleasant occurrence to this woman who was my distant cousin.

*****

From May 1945 through December of that same year I stayed with Peller and twenty-five other surviving Jews who lived in the large house he had acquired. During this time Jews throughout Poland were coming out of cellars and stables and various other hiding places and some were trying to reclaim property that was rightfully theirs. During the war many Poles had assumed ownership of these properties and had no desire to give them up.

In the city of Kielce about one hundred forty-five Jews survived the war. When they started reclaiming their property the Poles countered by starting a rumor that the Jews were holding Christian children as captives to use in pagan sacrifices. This was all the justification the superstitious Poles needed: riots started and in about the period of a week many of the surviving Jews were beaten to death. Some of the Jews who escaped this tragedy went to the Catholic priest who lived there and begged him to go on the radio and denounce the rumor and intervene on their behalf. Indeed he did go on the air, but what he said was: "I don't sympathize with the rioters. But the practice of blood libel has never been disproved, so I can do nothing."

In Gorlice the Poles took similar means of defending their usurped properties. Their disappointment that Jews didn't entirely disappear became obvious. Through the heart of the city flowed the river Ropa. The rumor spread that a Christian child had been killed and the body dumped under the bridge. Outside the Peller house a crowd gathered, yelling: "Kill the Jews!" Peller immediately called the police which were under Russian command. Now it just so happened that some of the Russian officers were Jewish. They had the police fire their guns into the air in order to disperse the mob. Peller, not wanting to let a potentially harmful situation simmer, pursued the story of the dead child. He traced it to a Polish prostitute whose child had died. She was paid to leave it under the bridge by the *Armja Krajowa* (land army), which was a reactionary partisan anti-Semitic group. Peller sued for prosecutions to be made and the Poles no longer had a convenient excuse to kill the Jews.

*****

There was considerable reconstruction going on in Gorlice and for living expenses and spending money I did odd jobs. I delivered things here and there, carried messages for the Russian military authority and performed chores on various farms. My travels often took me near the Padworski farm and I might have stopped in to see them had I not learned Peller had spoken to them about me and told them I was Jewish. Peller said they were not very surprised. But I was too ashamed to face them. Once, I caught sight of *Gospondyni* and I wanted to run to her. Mr. Padworski didn't look very well and I wanted to do something for him to show appreciation for the three long years of protection on his farm. Instead, I put my hand over my face so they couldn't see me and turned around, quickly walking in the opposite direction.

My duties as messenger boy for the Russian officers in charge of Gorlice put me in contact with some officers who were Jewish. The fact of their Jewishness they denied. Nevertheless,, they were appalled at the atrocities inflicted on the Jews during the war. They were among those Russian soldiers who liberated Auschwitz. They were particularly horrified at the complicity of some of the Polish informers who used to cripple and maim elderly Jewish women and men and then deliver them to the Gestapo tied together like sheep. Even though these Russians had no particular authority in the matter because there was now a newly constituted Polish government, they decided to pay a visit to a couple of these characters, including the two men called Lega and Krupa.

It was Peller who first told the officers about Lega and Krupa. They had been the ones responsible for the deaths of the Shiff brothers. Also, Krupa had discovered and turned in to the Gestapo the insane man who had escaped from the mass grave at Garbotz — the crazy man that the Jew Simcha had told me about.

First, Krupa denied he had ever done such things. Then, when he was beaten and almost blinded, he admitted his guilt and begged for mercy, saying he needed the money the Gestapo had given him for his family and that otherwise he wouldn't have done such things. He protested they had no right to beat him, that they had to go through the Polish courts and that he wanted his gentile, Christian lawyer. They kept repeating they were giving him the same justice he had given old man Menashi and many, many others. Of the deaths he was directly responsible for they reminded him, one by one.

Not too far from his house lived the woman named Polka who had had a Jewish lover. In fact, this lover was one of the Shiff brothers; and Krupa had betrayed them. The Germans had shot the lover right there in the house and made the woman bury him there. Krupa cringed when they went into the details. He got white and shaky and crouched low to the floor. Telling the story made them madder than they already were and one of the officers crippled the wretch Krupa with a blow to the head with his revolver.

So that was the end of a Polish traitor. His condition didn't bring to life those he had killed but there seemed some justice in it. One thing the war did was fill me with many conflicting emotions. Sometimes pity and compassion would emerge from me. Sometimes shame and extreme sorrow. Sometimes raw hatred.

In the town of Gorlice I was known as a "tough guy." I went around with a group of older boys who had survived the concentration camps and who had numbers burned into their arms, and if any peasant was treating a Jew badly we turned the tables. In December I managed to get an apartment of my own. There were a lot of empty houses but most of them were too run down to live in. This apartment was given to me by the now newly constituted Jewish Committee headed by Peller. It had lice and rats and no running water but it was inhabitable and the door even had a lock that worked. I was fifteen years old. Some of the boys I hung around with were in their early twenties and whenever they wanted to make love to some girl they would come to me and get the key to the apartment. "I'll be back in an hour or so," they would say, with a wink, and I felt vicariously a part of their adventures. These friends of mine included friendly Poles as well as Jews, and the girls they managed to pick up were peasants who came to town on market day with their fathers. In all of Gorlice there were only a couple Jewish girls left alive after the war. One of these girls stayed locked in her room all day long and never saw anyone. She had had a total mental breakdown.

I was proud to be such an important man associating with men and grownup boys. It was time when I looked forward to the future and thought perhaps the world would open up to me. One day I myself found an attractive peasant girl with very strong features. In order to get her to the apartment I had to bribe her with nylon stockings stolen from the black market. The apartment was broken down and roach infested, without running water or toilet — but then the living conditions of the peasants were't much better. The girl was interested in the stockings; I gave her the stockings, but since I lacked experience, I didn't get anywhere with her.

Several of my relatives were buried in different parts of the country. Some of the local peasants, who were by and large now willing to prove their friendliness to the Jews, encouraged my distant cousin, Oliner, to exhume the bodies for reburial in a Jewish cemetery. Peller also encouraged us to do this. In fact, on Garbotz, Peller was able to build a permanent memorial to the massacred people. The monument has the following inscription:

WTYN GROBIE MASOWYN
OTPOCZYWAJĄ, SZCZĄTKI OKOŁO
1000 ZYDÓW Z GORLIC I BOBOWEJ
OFIAR RZEŹI HITLEROWSKIEJ
ZAMORDOWANYCH BESTIALSKO W
DNIU 14 ŠIERPNIA 1942 ROKU
WYSTAWIENIE TEGO GROBU I
OPIEKA NAD TYM USWIĘCONYM
MIĘJSCU MARTYLOGII ŻYDOWSKIEJ
JEST GŁOWNA ZASŁUGA
OB. OB. NACHUMA ORMIANERA,
JAKUBA PELLERA PRZEDWODINCZĄCEGO
POWIATOWEGO KOMITETU
ŻYDOWSKIGO W GORLICACH

IN THIS MASS GRAVE
REST NEARLY 1000 JEWS
FROM GORLICE AND BOBOWA;
VICTIMS OF HITLERIAN BESTIAL SLAUGHTER
ON AUGUST 14, 1942.
THE ERECTION OF THIS MONUMENT
ON THIS HOLY GROUND
WAS DONE BY NACHUM ORMIANER,
AND JAKUB PELLER, THE CHAIRMAN OF THE
COUNTY JEWISH COMMITTEE OF GORLICE.

Lacking sufficient money for caskets, we made burial boxes of wood. A couple of the peasants helped us locate bodies and take them from the ground. The bodies were by this time rotted and the stench was awful. Nevertheless, we took them by horse and cart to the cemetary. Along the way, one time, I was arrested by the local police for not having permission to transfer human bodies. But I was soon released and we did succeed in the burial operation.

During this time Peller was also busy. Throughout the countryside he had traveled, along with others, gathering money in any conceivable manner. When he had accumulated a sufficient sum, he purchased gravestones and placed them at the

102

other mass graves in memory of the thousands of people buried there. Peller wore a pin striped suit, riding boots and felt hat and I envied him his strength and courage and leadership skills. Since the war I'd gone about reorganizing the ruin and chaos of my life, all the while trying to avoid confrontation with this place Garbotz, over which hung the particularly dark cloud of personal disaster. Surviving the war had required a certain sanity which was fragile indeed and I thought it couldn't withstand the blow of Garbotz. I was afraid — actually terrified — my cool demeanor would crack under the relentless stare of the spectre of brutal fate.

Sooner or later, of course, I had to visit Garbotz. There was the final resting place of part of my family, at least; and I went there with the naive hope of exhuming the bodies and giving them a decent burial. Imagine the desolate loneliness I experienced while standing in a little wood looking at a small meadow, knowing what lay underneath the grass! I cried out loud. I yelled to heaven. No one heard my yells except the tall trees. I looked up towards the heavens and thought perhaps my family was there. After all, I had been told that there is life after death. There was a breeze that day which lifted my hair and let it fall. The hopelessness of the task of ever retrieving the bodies overwhelmed me. My family had been taken from me. They were indistinguishable from the mass of a people diabolically slaughtered, and all I could be certain of was that I was a Jew. And yet, I thought, if I was a Jew, why wasn't I buried there with the rest of my people? As if in answer the breeze said nothing. Life was, in a sense, no more logical than death. There were no ready-made answers; and I had to live in order to discover why I survived one moment to the next. Before I left I started saying the *Kadish* (the prayer to the dead) . . . the few words that I remembered. I now felt suddenly good. The dead were at rest and my family forgave me for not dying with them. Peller constructed the beautiful stone and inscribed on it was the date and deed of the slaughter. I walked back to Gorlice feeling at peace with myself.

* * * * *

Gradually, an unrest stole over me. I became surly and quarreled with my friends. I got frustrated with my apartment and moved in with the surviving cousins. My cousin and her husband were only too happy to have me. At first I enjoyed their company. It felt good to be in a family situation once again where a man and a woman live together and make a home. But once again the unrest caught up with me.

I became frustrated with Gorlice, and when I thought of Poland in general a mild desperation gripped my mind. For me Poland was nothing but a graveyard. Some of my friends seemed to feel the same and we entertained the notion of leaving Poland. "Go west," we counseled each other. "Where there is opportunity, where there is an end to desolation and chaos." Of course, leaving Poland was easier said than done and many of my friends would obviously never make the move.

And perhaps I would not have made the move either had not Peller been in the habit of visiting the people I lived with. It became known to me that three of them were planning to leave Poland. They were going to journey west by looping through Germany and I decided to go with them, yet I felt really sorry for those that stayed behind in Poland. In fact, the plan of leaving gave me a great deal of satisfaction: the Germans had marched their armies through the Dukla Gap, and now I, a Jew, was going to walk on German soil.

The German mark was useless currency in Poland. Mere paper and readily available. In Germany, however, General Eisenhower (the Commander-in-Chief of Europe) had reinstated the value of the mark as legal tender. My three friends and I set about collecting marks and stuffing them into the false bottom of a suitcase. When we had gathered a few thousand of these marks we went to the Czechoslovakian border.

As it turned out Germany was already full of displaced persons and the border guard at the Czechoslovakian border turned us back. The money was still safe, hidden in the false bottom of the suitcase and we escaped by night into Czechoslovakia. Through this country we hitchhiked getting many rides from American GI's and in this way entered Germany.

My friends left me in a displaced persons' camp in Germany called Fernwald. When they were gone I knew they would not return and my future seemed bleak and empty of hope. Forsaken and forlorn, I greeted each day as if it were an unfaithful friend. Only the feeling of unrest which had first come over me in Gorlice spurred me on.

In the displaced persons' camp, food was very limited in supply. As in the ghetto, personal status was based on the amount of luxuries a person had and theft was common. I bummed around a lot and had some dealings with the black market. Many people were lost, wandering from camp to camp. I had no way of knowing if any of my family had survived the war. Very often I would take an American Army truck driven by black G.I.'s to the surrounding camps and search for possible relatives. Never did I find any relatives and the return to camp was often depressing.

The displaced persons' camp which was located near Munich needed some coal and I was asked to help in the operation. With a couple of men I went to the railroad station and we unloaded coal from a boxcar onto a truck. The truck was easily recognizable as a displaced persons' camp truck, and as we were driving towards Munich to make the delivery a German boy along the road started yelling, "Hey *Jude, Jude*." He was about my own age and I certainly understood that he meant, Jew, Jew, dirty Jew! My anger was so great I grabbed a piece of coal. I threw it at him and my aim by chance was so good that I hit him in the eye. And I felt good about it. Deep down inside me was a sadistic pleasure that I had managed to hurt the German.

The British government, with the help of the Jewish Refugee Committee of England, decided to accept several hundred refugee orphans from the camps throughout Germany. Since I had been unable to locate any surviving relatives, I signed up to go to England. After several weeks of waiting I decided one day to leave the camp and visit a friend of mine who was in another camp called Feldafing, near Munich, about sixty-four kilometers away. That very day the British Air Force planes arrived to pick up the boys who had signed up for England. Fortunately for me the fog was bad and the planes couldn't take off. Someone called up the camp I was visiting and they rushed me to the airport just in time to catch the flight.

In England we were greeted with great warmth and kindness by the British Jews and the government officials. We made the British newsreels. Only in England did life begin for me. In an old mansion, which served as a temporary youth hostel, I was one of hundreds of children given decent food, kindness, and the opportunity to rebuild my spirits. Education was made available to us and at the age of fifteen I took the first small step toward literacy. From about the age of nine, at which time the Germans first entered Dukla, until the age of fifteen, when they were driven out of Biesnik and defeated, I had lived in a state of darkness, in a state of uncertainty, in a state of primitivity, in a state which is a complete void; only filled with misery, with killings and bad memories. England in 1945 was like reaching paradise, to me.

ABOUT THE AUTHOR

The author is now an Associate Professor of Sociology at Humboldt State University, editor-in-chief of the *Humboldt Journal of Social Relations,* and has published articles in the area of race relations. His areas of interest are race and ethnic relations, social movements, and collective behavior. His current research deals with heroic altruism during World War II. He received his Ph.D. degree in Sociology from the University of California, Berkeley, in 1973.